# BUSHWHACKERS
*of the*
# BORDER

## The Civil War Period in Western Missouri

A SUMMARY AND APPRAISAL

By

## PATRICK BROPHY

VERNON COUNTY HISTORICAL SOCIETY

**BUSHWHACKER MUSEUM**

INC. NOT FOR PROFIT

NEVADA, MISSOURI

*i*

Cover Artwork
by Ed Koski

Second, Revised Edition
Copyright © 1980, 2000
Patrick Brophy

ISBN 1-893046-02-8

Library of Congress Catalog Card Number
00-132992

*Published by*
**VERNON COUNTY HISTORICAL SOCIETY**
« Bushwhacker Museum »
INC. NOT FOR PROFIT
231 North Main Street
Nevada, Missouri 64772

# TABLE OF CONTENTS

IKE SKELTON
4TH DISTRICT, MISSOURI

1404 LONGWORTH HOUSE OFFICE BUILDING
WASHINGTON, D.C.  20515
TELEPHONE (202) 225-2876

301 WEST LEXINGTON
ROOM NO 219
INDEPENDENCE, MISSOURI  64050
(816) 252-2560

319 SOUTH LAMINE
FEDERAL BUILDING
SEDALIA, MISSOURI  65301
(816) 826-2675

### Congress of the United States
### House of Representatives
#### Washington, D.C.  20515

August 19, 1980

With the strength of its writing and painstaking research, **Bushwhackers of the Border** has successfully reached into our past and brought to modern man's attention the flickering lamp of local history. The story of the Bushwhacker is dynamic and colorful. It is a chronicle of our ancestors at war during a national crisis.

The author, Patrick Brophy, has effectively incorporated an important part of any local, American or world history...that is, the land around us. Too often, historians overlook this important element, but not Mr. Brophy. History cannot be intelligently studied without constant reference to the geographical surroundings which affect it. Mr. Brophy knows the land in which this history is based, and we, the readers, benefit from this knowledge.

**Bushwhackers of the Border** is a glass through which you and I may see with ancestral eyes, not only the various deeds of the local past, which were sometimes brutal and occasionally heroic, but also the different men and women who had roles in the making of this local history.

IKE SKELTON
Member of Congress

*iv*

# ONE
## *The Border*

The Missouri-Kansas border is no ordinary state line. For longer than any other it was *the* Border—with a capital *B*—the would-be "permanent frontier" between Western civilization and the Stone Age. For a decade it was the battle-line between North and South. For decades more it divided East from West. Even today it lingers, the seam between subtly dissimilar societies.

America has known other "borders"; but oftenest the word has meant the *frontier*—in the sense not of a line but of a place, or even "a form of society." In the beginning, "the Border" was but shorthand for "the *Indian* Border": the edge of settlement, beyond which lay raw nature and savagery. Unlike such synonyms as "boundary," notes Walter Prescott Webb, "border" implies violence.

*The* Border, then—along with "Border warfare"—came ashore with the first landfalling white men, and came West with their descendants. Revolutionary War days found it, more or less stalled, along the Appalachian chain. Over the next half-century, slow but sure, it climbed and fought its way across. Then, at the outer edges of soon-to-be Missouri and Arkansas, it stalled again—and *stayed* stalled for over thirty years; indeed, in a sense, forever.

1

For this time the *place* itself was different, something entirely new in pioneer experience. The *mountains* had proven unable to stem the settlement tide for long; for the country was pretty much the same on one side as on the other. Getting over might be a trick, but once across, the world was still the old familiar place.

The *prairies,* on the other hand, while offering no comparable physical barrier, posed a psychological one actually tougher to surmount. When the pioneers first reached the timbered country's western limit, as a litterateur puts it, "they came out into the light, stood blinking at the flat and featureless immensity spread before them, where there were no logs to build cabins or churches, no rails for fences, none of the game whose ways they knew." For this, nothing in their past, racial or personal, had prepared them. Northern Europe, whence their forebears and their culture had come, was a place of majestic, storybook forests. Trees—once even objects of worship—were simply the furniture of the world as they knew it. And here in this New World, nothing had so characterized and conditioned the spread of their way of life, the growth of their new nation, as the struggle with, and dependence upon, the forest, the "Back Woods," as it was called: that timbered hinterland ever "back there" to the West. In all their folklore and history, they literally couldn't see the forest for the trees. American democracy itself, according to Frederick Jackson Turner, came "stark and strong and full of life from the American forest."

And yet here, deep in the continent, the trees abruptly thinned, grew stunted—and then were no more. And so those doughty axe-wielding first comers fresh from the taming of a thousand miles of forest for the first time ever turned back—"cowered back into the shade"—and for the last time ever settled down to felling trees and raising log-cabin dwellings, farming "the margins of the prairies like a timid bather testing the water with his toe"—this shore, so to speak, of the familiar wooded world, overlooking that sea of grass, fascinating perhaps but "of course uninhabitable by a people depending upon agriculture for their subsistence."

Americans got over their preconceptions about prairies, of course, but it took them fully a third of a century, and the effects of their long hesitation bedevil us yet. "An institutional *fault,* comparable to a geological fault," notes Walter Prescott Webb, runs "from middle Texas to Illinois or Dakota." Here "the ways of life and of

2

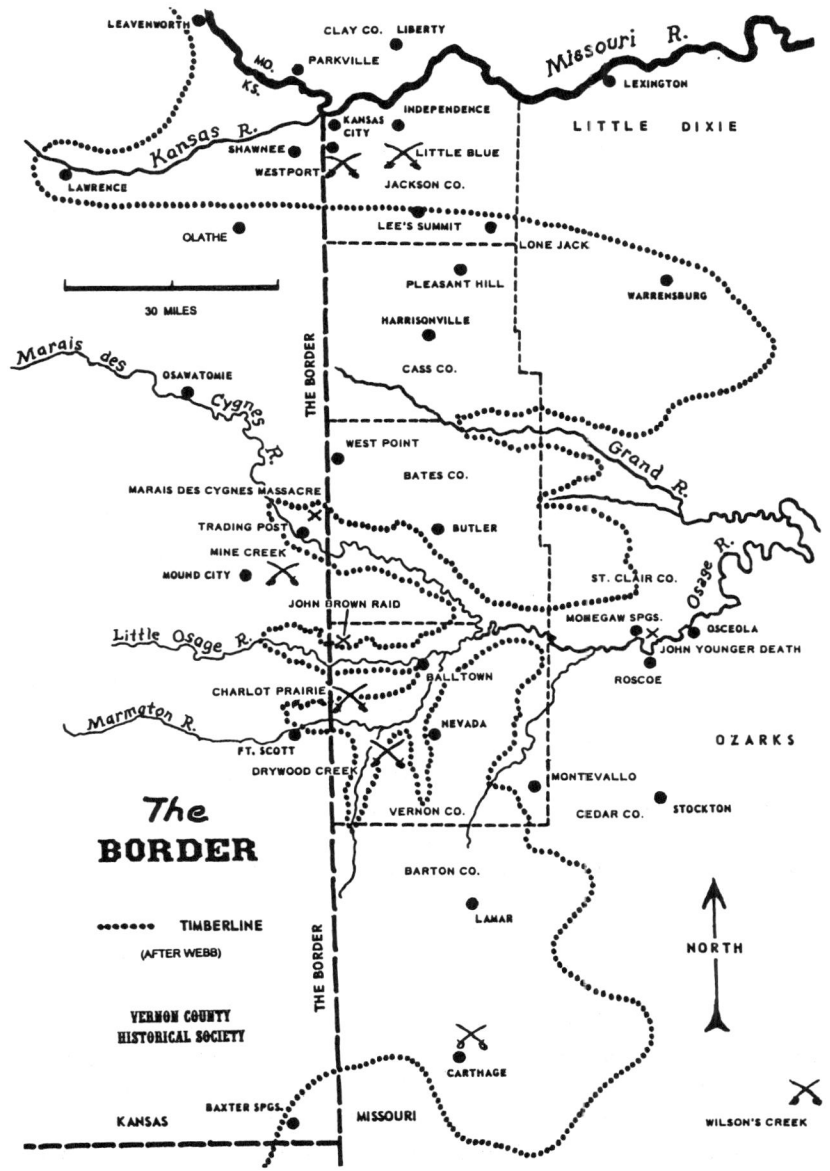

LEAVENWORTH
CLAY CO. LIBERTY
PARKVILLE
MO.
KS.
Missouri R.
LEXINGTON
LITTLE DIXIE
Kansas R.
KANSAS CITY
INDEPENDENCE
SHAWNEE
WESTPORT
LITTLE BLUE
JACKSON CO.
LAWRENCE
OLATHE
LEE'S SUMMIT
LONE JACK

30 MILES

PLEASANT HILL
WARRENSBURG
HARRISONVILLE

Marais des
Cygnes R.
OSAWATOMIE
THE BORDER
CASS CO.

WEST POINT
Grand R.
BATES CO.

MARAIS DES CYGNES MASSACRE
TRADING POST
BUTLER
MINE CREEK
MOUND CITY
ST. CLAIR CO.
Osage R.
JOHN BROWN RAID
MOMEGAW SPGS.
OSCEOLA
Little Osage R.
JOHN YOUNGER DEATH
CHARLOT PRAIRIE
BALLTOWN
ROSCOE
Marmaton R.
NEVADA
OZARKS
FT. SCOTT
DRYWOOD CREEK
MONTEVALLO
VERNON CO.
CEDAR CO.
STOCKTON

The
BORDER
BARTON CO.

•••••• TIMBERLINE
(AFTER WEBB)
LAMAR
NORTH

VERNON COUNTY
HISTORICAL SOCIETY
THE BORDER

KANSAS
BAXTER SPGS.
MISSOURI
CARTHAGE
WILSON'S CREEK

3

living changed. Practically every institution that was carried across was either broken and remade or else greatly altered."

The "institutional fault" simply mirrored a natural one. It was the human accommodation to the *timberline:* nature's great divide between woodlands and prairies. Hardly a true, clearcut "line," of course, it was rather a gradual giving-way of trees to grass over many miles. And clearing, plowing, and other human interferences have worse-blurred the original, already blurry line the settlers found. Ah, but it's still there. If the interferences ceased tomorrow, the trees would start to reclaim their old domain, while yielding their gains to the resurgent grass. Drawn on a map, the timberline is, obviously, both an oversimplification and an anachronism.

Missouri, then, lies—or lay—in the *Eastern Woodlands,* while Iowa and eastern Kansas lie in the *Prairie Plains:* the *Tall Grass Country,* as differentiated from the *Plains Proper,* or *Short Grass Country,* farther West ("prairie" is merely treeless; "plains" are treeless, hill-less, and waterless). Even today Missouri is 34 percent forest, Kansas a bare two percent. Roughly, the timberline follows Missouri's northern and western edges; farther south it straggles off westward through eastern Oklahoma and middle Texas.

The people the pioneers found living along the timberline, it seems, not only had made their own adjustments to it but shared the newcomers' ambiguities about it. "The Osage culture," writes Carl H. Chapman, "though it has been very difficult to classify, can be considered to be representative of Indian culture in a border area. Their cultural situation reflects the border position of the tribe both physiographically and culturally." Tribal tradition and modern scholarship alike suggest that the Osages had moved into their namesake river valley from somewhere to the east or north—timbered country—and they clung to their semi-permanent villages just within the timber, not yet quite at home or at ease on the prairies. And while on the hunt they lived in portable skin tents, like those of the true, nomadic Plains tribes, their home dwellings—more or less permanent lodges of poles, brush, and bark—clearly pointed to their forest past. Still in many ways the prairies had become home to them. In 1755, when some Osages joined the Woodland tribes in a far-eastern white man's war, they complained of the Woodlanders' "cowardly" habit of fighting from concealment! "They found it difficult to remain behind their trees and their windfalls," writes

4

Osage historian John Joseph Mathews. "Plains fighting was much more dramatic certainly, as compared with the panther-stealth and hunting-cat seriousness of the forest fighting."

And human destiny had been even more decisively influenced by the timberline in the endless times before the Osages. Lacking the horse—that latecomer—earlier Indians faced an almost insuperable barrier in the Plains. The prehistoric Indian cultural tradition perhaps most characteristic of Missouri is called by archeologists—what else?—the "Woodland."

White American familiarity with the Border region began with Captain Zebulon M. Pike, its first official American visitor, whose impressions appeared in print four years after his expedition up the Osage River and out over the Plains in the summer of 1806. "Pike," asserts Webb, "left a record which is more valuable to the student of life on the Plains than that of Lewis and Clark."

"From the Missouri to the head of the Osage River," Pike wrote, "the country will admit of a numerous, extensive, and compact population; from thence on . . . it appears to me to be possible only to introduce a limited population." He sings the praises of future western Missouri: "hilly, but well timbered"; "heavy timber"; "well-timbered, rich soil, and very proper for the cultivation of all the productions of our middle and western states."

Farther west, however—beyond the Osage villages—his appraisal suffers a sea-change: "The view on the prairies becomes unbounded"; "high and gravelly ridges of prairie land"; "prairie hills, affording not more than sufficient timber for firewood for a limited number of inhabitants for a few years"; "very little timber, prairies high and dry"; "the borders of woodland" along the streams "are no more than a line traced on a sheet of paper"; and finally, most damning of all, "here the country is very deficient of water."

For Missouri, then, Pike foresaw a bounteous re-creation of his boyhood Ohio. For the place not yet named Kansas—where even the firewood wouldn't last fifteen years—he held out the hope of, at best, a few squalid mud huts "like those in New Spain."

The first Osage treaty, negotiated in 1808 as a sequel to Pike's visit, took its cue from his report. While giving white men the solidly wooded bulk of Missouri, it absentmindedly left the Osages the pleasant transition-zone itself, the future "Border tier" of Missouri counties, wherein lay all their traditional villages.

The onrush of white settlement and the climate of frontier politics made the tribe's early eviction from all Missouri inevitable; but the Osages themselves unwittingly hastened the process, when a tribal delegation, visiting Washington in 1820, reportedly asked "to have missionaries sent among them."

Clearly such Indian requests—by no means uncommon—were getting "a little twisted in the telling." Religion, to the Indians (as, indeed, originally to everybody), meant worldly power: the ability "to influence other people and other beings." To many "it was apparent that the Anglo-Americans were simply more powerful and that the Indians' sacred powers had failed them." They "sought to decipher the secrets of Anglo-American strength"—"not the Americans' religion but rather the skills they needed to interact successfully with Americans." They failed to grasp (as indeed did most whites themselves) that white power derived not from religion but rather from natural science, often hostile to all religion. Blindly the missionaries brought word of the *next* world to Indians whose thoughts were very much on *this* one. The white faith, exulted Big Soldier on arrival of the Harmony Mission party among the Osages, "'would teach them how to make corn soft.' He also inquired whether any of us knew how to make [gun]powder"!

Missouri, of course, had had white settlements in her eastern reaches for nearly a century; but the forty-odd Protestant missionaries and their dependents who came out in 1821, the very year of Missouri's statehood, marked the start of permanent white settlement anywhere on the Border beyond the big rivers.

Harmony Mission, planted near the Big and Little Osage river junction, not far from the tribal villages, was typical of Indian missions: a  failure, judged in terms of its stated aims—indeed, actually frustrating them by opening the country to other whites. Frontiersmen—lay employees and hangers-on—grew familiar with this inviting scrap of Osage land lying just within the timber, with inevitable consequences.  Meanwhile, the Osages proved distressingly resistant to both civilizing and Christianizing.  Like other Indians exposed to white influences, they were growing restless and dissatisfied. "Chiefs and sensible men among the tribes, to a great extent, feel that a change in their situation has become necessary"; their "existence as a distinct people depends on their migrating." "Traditionalists felt the promising twin pulls of better hunting and isolation from white settlers." Long before the Treaty of 1825 ratified their final removal from Missouri, many Osages had already left voluntarily for modern Kansas or Oklahoma.

The "Indian question" was a national problem. The Rev. Isaac McCoy, founder of the Shawnee Mission in Johnson County, Kansas, and the Rev. Jedidiah Morse, engaged by the secretary of war in 1822 to investigate and report on Indian affairs, were among the many decent, thoughtful whites who by 1830 had concluded that efforts to "civilize" the Indians had failed, that the one hope for the demoralized Eastern tribes lay in their migration to the West, away from contaminating white influences—"the only practicable course which can be pursued," Morse called it. Thomas Jefferson himself had entertained the idea of setting aside at least Upper Louisiana Territory (i.e. Missouri) as a giant Indian reservation.

The rapid white settlement of the territory's timbered eastern portions, of course, relegated that idea to the realm of fantasy; but the rump, so to speak, of the notion rang increasingly sound. Pike had come back full of grave doubts about the value—to white men —of the lands beyond Missouri; and as time passed other explorers were pulling even longer faces. The "Great American Desert" idea had existed since Spanish days; but it was the observations of Colonel Stephen H. Long and members of his 1819 dry-season expedition that truly brought it home to Americans.

For Long, the Plains region bore "a resemblance to the deserts of Siberia." "I do not hesitate in giving the opinion that it is almost wholly unfit for cultivation," he opined. "The scarcity of wood and water, almost uniformly prevalent, will prove an insuperable obstacle in the way of settling the country." His associate Edwin James agreed: The lack of wood and water rendered the country "an unfit residence for any but a nomade [sic] population."

Long added, significantly: "This region, however, viewed as a frontier, may prove of infinite importance to the United States, inasmuch as it is calculated to serve as a barrier to prevent too great an extension of our population westward."

Pike had sounded the same note: "Our citizens being so prone to rambling and extending themselves on the frontier will, through necessity, be constrained to limit their extent on the west to the borders of the Missouri and Mississippi, while they leave the prairies . . . to the wandering and uncivilized aborigines."

7

Quaint as they may sound to us, such notions were not altogether fanciful. "There were no plows in the country capable of turning over and reducing the thick, tough sod," notes a Missouri historian. "The plows in vogue at that day were usually composed of cast-iron points and wooden mold-boards, and were only of service in loose soil." One of the Harmony Mission party wrote home that the plows they'd brought out with them were "soon broken in pieces by the strong roots of the prairie grass." "The share must be kept so thin and sharp that steel, hardened or unhardened, breaks and wears into notches, against the wirey edge of the grass roots." The taming of the prairies would have to await advances in agricultural technology—most notably the steel plow perfected by John Deere of Moline in the 1840s and 1850s.

Policymakers lost no time in taking the explorers' hint. John C. Calhoun, President Monroe's secretary of war (the Bureau of Indian Affairs, established only in 1824, remained under the War Department till 1848), commissioned studies by Morse and others and endorsed their recommendations. The secretary's report to the president, transmitted to Congress on January 27, 1825, became the cornerstone of the Indian removal policy.

For the good both of the Indians and of the nation, its cohesion and stability, Calhoun summed up, some limit must be placed on the white population's dispersion, the frontier's headlong westward advance. And the obvious place for that limit was the eastern edge of that "desert" so "unsuitable for civilized occupation."

Calhoun proposed the establishment of a line, running north from the Mexican border along the western borders of Arkansas and Missouri and thence to and along the Mississippi to its source, to be known as the *Indian line.* White settlement would be permitted only east of the line; the country to the west of it would be permanently reserved for the Indians, natives and immigrants.

The line would take the shape of a chain of forts, to keep settlers and Indians apart and at peace. In places, settlement was already approaching the line, and in 1825, at just the right moment, the hardheaded Osages cashed in, bowed to the inevitable and joined their kin on the Neosho, in southeast Kansas, already well on their way toward being the wealthiest Indians.

But other tribes were proving stubborner. The Black Hawk War of 1832, centered in northern Illinois and Wisconsin, gave the whole

8

frontier a scare. And in the shorter run even the Osages fell on relatively hard times in their new Kansas homes and began finding the new Missouri settlements an irresistible temptation. In March, 1838, a tiny band, hungry and homesick, strayed back over the line and slew a few hogs and a lone settler, sparking a statewide panic grandiosely dubbed "the Osage War," and a draconian expulsion order enforced against all Indians still living in the state, even those married to whites. And just a month later President Martin Van Buren ordered General Winfield Scott to use force to move the Cherokees, the largest and stubbornest Eastern tribe, from their Georgia homeland to the new "Indian Territory," then comprising not only today's Oklahoma but also Kansas and Nebraska. They passed through southern Missouri; though the lachrymose term "Trail of Tears" was coined only in modern times.

Bit by bit, then, the Border was sketched in. Military posts large and small sprang up along a zigzag thousand-mile line south-by-southwest from Fort Snelling—afterwards Minneapolis—to the Sabine Pass on the Gulf of Mexico. The line grew from the ends, starting with Fort Smith on the Arkansas River in 1817 and Fort Snelling on the Mississippi in 1819, followed in 1824 by Forts Gibson and Towson on the Arkansas and Red rivers respectively, then Fort Leavenworth on the Missouri in 1827. The line soon lost its significance south of the Red River as it became plain that tall-timbered East Texas, willynilly, would be white man's country.

The stratetic 250-mile central stretch between Gibson and Leavenworth was both the least-defined by natural features and the last to be fortified. In 1836 President Jackson signed legislation for the building of a road between the two posts; construction contracts were let late in 1838. Almost exactly on the Border and paralleling it, the route became known as the Great Military Road or even more sarcastically the "Whiskey Road" as traders selling whiskey to the Indians soon found it far more useful than the army.

Not till 1842 (by which time the Indian removal was virtually completed) was a commission sent out to pick a site for the fort needed to plug the final gap and shield southwest Missouri "against the depredations of the western Indians." The commissioners sought the advice of Colonel George Douglass, first settler (1834) on the Marmaton River near modern Deerfield. He told them of a low bluff lying in "unbroken prairie" just outside the state and on Federal land, some ten miles west of his "plantation" in the timbered Marmaton bottoms. And so, one April morning in 1842, accompanied by Douglass and Abraham Redfield, another pioneer settler, the commissioners rode over into future Kansas and laid out Fort Scott, naming it for the general. Oddly—ominously—they faced it east, away from the Indians—back toward Missouri.

The frontier society taking shape behind the Border, "though it had a sectional character of its own, had extremely close links with the South." "Up to the third decade of the century," anywhere along the frontier, "New Englanders remained small islands in a sea of Southern folk." Harmony Mission formed just such an island, being soon surrounded by transplanted Kentuckians and Tennesseans. A local historian is at pains to assure us, however, that they "were not rough, uncouth, ignorant backwoodsmen, who subsisted entirely by hunting, were clothed in buckskin, and didn't know a letter in the book." "The old rough, unlettered pioneers of Kentucky and Tennessee had but few counterparts among the early settlers here."

An uneasy blend of the old, aristocratic Tidewater and the raw, "rugged-individualist" Scotch-Irish world of the Appalachian backwoods, this Southern frontier culture spread like wildfire. Hardly had it reached the "western waters"—the easternmost feeders of the Ohio-Mississippi—than it seemed to be everywhere at once; "western Georgia and northern Florida were not opened until central Missouri was being settled." Both halves of the Southern personality, so to speak, came West; though oddly they "traded places" enroute. Scotch-Irish "hillbillies" claimed mountainous southern Missouri; while genteel planters from the riverine or lower South put up their proud, pillared mansions and set their slaves to tilling the rich fields along the great rivers of the state's northern half; in Missouri the Deep South—"Little Dixie"—is to the north.

The two groups had different interests; but their battles for political control (with victory going, for the time being, to the planting "aristocracy") were muted by the key thing they shared. Always conservatives, Missourians rich and poor were passionately attached to the pioneer or Southern ideal of independence and self-sufficiency, personal and communal. The vast majority—yeoman farmers—opposed "the older, would-be aristocracy of slaveholders," but even more "the market economy spreading from the Northeast." To that economy's disturbing new ideals of "industrialization, urbanization, education, and personal orderliness and accumulation" "they counterposed their personal freedom and private property, community cooperation and family honor." "Yet at the same time, most Missourians would not have minded getting rich. They longed for profitable contacts with an outer world which interested them even as it repelled them."

But the stresses and strains of these economic and social changes still lay largely hidden in the future. Indeed, from the other side of the terrible war brought on largely by those changes, Missourians justly would look back on those first days of statehood—"the halcyon frontier days"—as a golden age. "In those early years, Missouri seemed to enjoy a happy combination of the splendors of nature and the heroics of men." For a moment, freedom and security, the old self-sufficiency and the new market affluence, the contradictions of human nature itself almost, had struck a balance. Here even Daniel Boone found elbow-room enough. The fur trade and the Santa Fe Trail commerce—both fairly Missouri monopolies—epitomized the state's unique marriage of rugged-individualism and market-savvy cooperativeness.

No longer annually creeping farther West, the Border became fixed—a way of life, a state of mind. For over thirty years Missouri was the nation's western "shore." "A solid, rooted society of forty years dwelled here on splendid farms and plantations, rich in cattle, horses, and mules, with black slaves hoeing fields of corn, tobacco, and hemp. Green-lawned courthouses surrounded by thriving, white-fenced towns dotted the countryside. Everything bespoke plenty. And even though the Missouri border was in many respects crude, rough, and unmistakably Western, it was like another world when compared to the land over the line."

"Over the line" lay another world altogether. There rolled the boundless prairie sea where, surely, adventure and riches awaited the dauntless terrestrial mariner—and for which maritime law was even being seriously proposed. Santa Fe traders, tensely and uncomfortably homecoming over the Indian-ridden blank of future Kansas, found themselves looking forward longingly to "the States"—to genial, cosmopolitan Missouri. Backwoods Missourians warily searched for strayed stock over in that "Indian Territory" bare steps from their snug, safe hearthsides. A generation arose, flourished, and died, and knew no other way.

11

Men had begun to lose sight of the fact that the timberline—the Border's basis in nature—itself had no true, tidy clarity. A straight line arbitrarily drawn on the map had taken on its own overriding, intimidating reality. East of the line lay all the comfortable, rough-and-ready panoply of the pioneer's world; west of the line, the Stone Age—and a Stone Age now debauched by civilization, doubly dangerous. Waylaid east of the line, you did what you would today: rushed to the sheriff, and then confidently sat back while the wheels of justice creaked and clanked. West of the line—alas! There was no sheriff, the U. S. marshal had other business, doubtless hundreds of miles away, the country belonged to the Indians anyhow, you were a mere trespasser, and your assailant, if not a trespasser himself, was but a Redman righteously doing his thing.

The trespassers, though, were multiplying. Clear back in 1825, at Council Grove, the government had duly treated with the Osages for the safe passage of the overland trails. But the trails must be serviced; the servicers themselves, with their dependents, must be fed, sheltered, protected—almost unnoticed this chain reaction became settlement for its own sake. The folk-tales about the forbidding Great American Desert west of Missouri continued to be told, but they were ringing ever hollower. Whereas "for the multitudes the tradition that the country to the west of the Missouri River was good only for the Indians and of no value to the whites was still sound doctrine, many people knew better."

Explorer John C. Fremont, in 1843, became the first authority to reverse his predecessors' judgment in cold print, rehabilitating their hostile wastes as "a vast territory lying open to interested settlers." And almost overnight the revolutionary thesis grew matter-of-fact. Just a year later Santa Fe trader Josiah Gregg could enthuse:

"All who have traversed these delightful regions look forward with anxiety to the day when the Indian title to the land shall be extinguished and flourishing white settlements dispel the gloom which at present prevails over this uninhabited region."

# TWO
## *"Border Ruffians"*

In the ordinary course of events, Missouri would now—almost unnoticed—have begotten Kansas, just as, in an earlier time, Kentucky and Tennessee had begotten Missouri. America had always grown in this contiguous, "organic" manner; "settlers moved west pretty much along parallels of latitude."

But times were no longer "ordinary." The frontier march had lost its stride; and during its thirty-year hesitation the world had become quite a different place. The pioneers of 1821 were in their dotage, if not in their graves; and for their children "the old fiction of the Great American Desert was not yet fully discredited." The economics of emigration were stacked against them. For Missouri's leading men made their living planting cotton, hemp, tobacco; their capital was tied up in the slave-gangs needed to produce these intensive, lowland crops unadaptable to parched, upland Kansas. "The Great Plains presented a barrier, which arrested for a time the whole westward movement," notes Webb, "but the barrier was greater for the South than for the North."

Even so, most "first Kansans" were footloose Missourians, blazers and servicers of the overland trails, all of which struck off from the great bend of the Missouri River near modern Kansas City. "Missourians had genuine and traditional interests in Kansas. The old Santa Fe trail . . . had played an important part both in the material and spiritual development of Missouri. The Kansas plains had linked market and supply and the wheels of heavily laden Missouri wagons had left deep scars upon those plains to witness possession by the right of conquest. Service to Indian missions across the border and trade with the tribes and military posts had strengthened the claim. Rightly the Missouri farmer, with the usual Western restlessness, looked across the border and dreamed of the day when he might move again, into fresh new lands. Kansas was his particular domain. It belonged to him as new lands had traditionally belonged to settlers nearest their borders."

But interest in the prairies was no longer limited to neighbors. Almost overnight, the 1849 gold rush turned the trickle of overland travel to a torrent. California soared to statehood in a single year; travel to Oregon and Utah mushroomed. Between the old Border and the new far-Western settlements lay up to 2,400 dusty, rocky, dangerous miles in which wagon-tracks evanesced like contrails. Still the wagons came on; and now and then, here and there, a wagon stopped. There were hapless westerers who just fell by the wayside, to eke out their future catering to the luckier. And there were the Josiah Greggs—those who simply fell in love with "these delightful regions." Northeasterners in particular seemed drawn—doubtless by the sheer challenge. Kansas posed far less a contrast to bleak, rock-ribbed New England than lush, muggy Missouri, cradled in the arms of earth's mightiest river.

Increasing settlement made urgent the need for organized government west of the Border—seemingly a simple problem but one complicated by the biggest change that had come over the country in the preceding thirty years: the deepening sectional disagreement over the westward spread of slavery.

The question had reared its head even back in 1820 during the debates over Missouri's own admission to the Union. The Missouri Compromise, prohibiting further slave states north of the line of Missouri's southern boundary, was thought to have buried the issue peaceably and permanently—an illusion the contiguous westward movement's thirty-year halt had served to reinforce. But Southerners—finding themselves increasingly on the defensive nationwide—

14

chafed under the symbolism, if not the reality, of the restriction. Missourians especially saw it as a wrongful infringement of their time-honored pioneering right to move west as and when they would, taking their institutions—including the "peculiar" one, slavery—along. "Kansas was destined to be an economic dependency of Missouri," they argued. "Whether Kansas was a free or slave state would make little difference in this basic situation."

Against such practical reasonings a small but growing minority in the North had begun to oppose the moral argument: Slavery was wrong; therefore, even if its extinction wasn't possible quite yet, clearly the time had come to draw a line against its further spread; and the natural place for that line was—the Border.

Early in 1854, seeking to break the deadlock, Illinois Senator Stephen A. Douglas introduced his Kansas-Nebraska Bill, with its provision that "all questions of slavery in the territories . . . are to be left to the decision of the people residing therein."

The South welcomed the proposal; and Westerners too hailed it "not as a disruptive measure or a triumph for the slave interests but as an equitable means of allowing the territories to care for their own affairs." Yet many Northeasterners seethed with outrage. For almost the first time radical antislavery views, heretofore confined to a "lunatic fringe," approached respectability. In Michigan and Wisconsin a new grassroots party, the Republican, took shape, pledged against any extension of slavery. The Massachusetts legislature chartered an Emigrant Aid Society "to win Kansas from the 'horseback chawbacks' of the border."

Douglas, the "chawbacks," moderates everywhere were surprised and shocked at the shrill reaction. Historically America had lived at peace with slavery. North and South "had not disagreed initially as to the position of the Negro in American society." "Slavery as a question of ethics was not the fundamental issue in the years preceding the bombardment of Fort Sumter." It was righteous abolitionism that was new and strange—part guilty conscience, perhaps, among New England families retired on the boodle of the slave-trade; part the new, secular faith in salvation through social reform—*any* social reform—that was rapidly replacing the region's once-so-vigorous otherworldly religion. Often animated less by concern for the slaves, it seemed, than by an irrational hatred of their fellow-countrymen who owned them, and of a nation and a

Constitution that sanctioned slavery, abolitionists saw in the Kansas-Nebraska Bill a disgraceful, disastrous retreat from the moral high ground painfully carved out in the Missouri Compromise—a diabolical triumph for slavery. It was widely agreed the "peculiar institution" stood scant chance on the prairies; if the South had won, in other words, "Kansas would have presented the strange spectacle of a slave state without slaves!" Thus at most the Kansas-Nebraska Bill was a substanceless sop to a South ever more on the losing end. Far from content with this substantial edge, however, abolitionists put forth the "conspiracy theory": The nation stood in imminent peril from the wicked aggressions of the "Slave Power."

And not satisfied simply to denounce slavery, they assailed in the bitterest, most intemperate terms those among whom, through no particular fault of their own, it now existed—those "'horseback chawbacks' of the border," "quintessential 'poor white trash' . . . they attacked the innermost character of all Missourians."

Missourians and other Southerners responded as those under attack usually do. Answering extremism with an extremism of their own, they were soon coming to see proposals for even reasonable curbs on slavery as intolerable discriminations against their whole way of life—pious pretexts for Northern imperialism.

Northern hypocrisy, as Southerners saw it, spoke for itself. Abolitionists decried Southern "racism" while maintaining time-honored racial relations in the North and West; they warned of the "Africanizing" of the West, and called for "free soil for free [i.e. white] men." As freestate Kansans' exclusion law (one of the first laws they were to pass) would seem to prove beyond all denying, they "did not want Negroes there." "In their so-called Topeka Constitution the Kansas Republicans *forbade free Negroes even to come into the state* [italics in source]." "It was not bondage that troubled them—it was the negro, free or slave." "The abolitionist wishes to abolish slavery . . . because he wishes to abolish the black man," Emerson privately conceded. Southerners differed only in favoring the more traditional means of racial control—slavery.

At the same time they wanted to be free to move west, into the new lands they'd helped win for the nation, bringing their lawful property with them, property the Constitution permitted—the Constitution their ancestors had embraced only on that solemn understanding, then disputed by none. To close a territory to such property was simply to close it to Southerners—assuring the forming of a new "free state" to further shrink the South's fading parity in the Senate, that last bulwark of sectional balance. The South had surrendered California; she was closing her eyes to the North's grabbing of Nebraska virtually by stealth—for all seemed to forget that the Kansas-Nebraska Bill provided for *two* territories, not just one, and Southerners felt an equal division had been implied. In their growing desperation it was unthinkable that Kansas, too, should be lost, Missouri's edge in the migration race undercut by a handful of hysterical, canting Yankee schoolmarms!

Missourians themselves had even urgenter reasons for alarm. Already Missouri was the most vulnerable slave state. If Northerners took Kansas, her isolation would be total. Severed from her sisters by rivers and hills, she'd be left "sticking up like a sore thumb" into politically hostile territory; "on every hand slaves would be running away, and anti-slavery sentiment rilling through the dam."

And so easygoing old Missouri roused to her twin duties, as she saw them, of regional loyalty and sheer self-defense, taking the fateful first steps down a dark road. "High excitement prevailed"; the Border saw "recruitings, organization of companies, drills, armings, as if some great military expedition was afoot." No affair of the "fringe," of riffraff or out-of-control mobs, it was a communal, "mainstream" movement, led by the state's "most prominent politcal figures"—such soon-to-be immortals as Jo Shelby and Claiborne Jackson. For Missouri was an articulated, hierarchic society whose "dregs" knew its place—it was in chaotic Kansas, by contrast, that "dregs" would rise to the top! Most journalism of the period would have us conclude that Benjamin Stringfellow, early spokesman of the Missouri cause—and the state's ex-attorney general—was an ignorant, demagogic nobody. Northern publicists strove hard to portray David R. Atchison, the state's leading pro-slaveryite, as an unprincipled boor. Granted this admired veteran president pro-tem of the U. S. Senate inspired a meeting of his Platte County constituents to resolve "that if the territory be opened to settlement, we pledge ourselves to each other to extend the institutions of Missouri over the territory at whatever sacrifices of blood and treasure." Yet Atchison's actions seem to have been far more temperate than his words, and his biographer—no partisan—concedes him to have been actually a moderating influence.

The abolitionists had struck first—Missourians felt—with their rabid rhetoric and "aid societies": "unholy combinations in New England to ship rowdies and vagabonds to Kansas with Bibles in one hand and rifles in the other." Missourians dared not await the territory's legal opening. In early spring many crossed into Kansas, staked claims on land technically still belonging to the Indians, organized self-defensive associations to assure member rights, and returned home for the summer—all time-honored pioneering practices. When the first Massachusetts men arrived, in late July, they found the best spots blanketed with claimstakes, and arms-bristling Missourians defiantly guarding their absent comrades' rights.

On election day in November the absentees returned in force —and chose a Tennessean territorial delegate to Congress. The next year, as freesoilers hesitantly dug in their heels, the Missourians crushed them by numbers and timely doses of muscle. Some 5,000 of the 6,000 votes were cast by Missourians. Kansas awoke with a territorial legislature full of Missourians. The freesoilers looked to Washington to disavow the election; but to their amazement President Franklin Pierce shrugged complaints aside: "The much-maligned Missouri invaders were legitimate settlers"; "these people had their rights." Indeed, the Missourians saw themselves as far more nearly "residents" of Kansas than Easterners sent out at the expense of third parties with political axes to grind, carbine-armed by gullible or hypocritical church congregations.

The tragic flaw in Douglas's doctrine of "squatter sovereignty," as it had come to be called, stood revealed. By neglecting to define "resident" the Kansas-Nebraska Act became a gilt-edged invitation to ballot-box-stuffing—to deliberate "packing" of the territory with mercenary "settlers" hired out of Missouri doggeries or Chicago "joints"—for these were games two sides could play, and were playing. And there were more Northerners to play them.

As "hired guns" and opportunists replaced honest idealists or simple homesteaders among the freesoil rank-and-file, men of "the most fanatic and vicious temperament" were rising to lead them. To their wild-eyed faces the poised, patrician ones of the Missouri chiefs present a telling contrast. Compare serene Shelby or Jackson, for instance, with snaky, Cassius-like Lane or Montgomery!

In large part the Kansas disorders were simply the kinds of things that always happened in a new territory, for crass, all-too-human motives having nothing whatever to do with politics or ideals, and were happening at the same time in Nebraska, where slavery wasn't an issue at all. But the world ignored Nebraska; the press had eyes only for poor "Bleeding Kansas" and her bloody-handed assailant, Missouri. "Each clash was magnified by the nation's press into a struggle between the forces of slavery and freedom." That both sides sinned, that both had their villains, none denies. "Both contained an unhealthy sprinkling of cutthroats attracted by the promise of trouble." And yet one side reaped virtually all the blame. For there was one all-important difference between them, hardly remarked either at the time or since.

"There were many men of real literary ability" among the freesoilers. "Every prominent Northern Republican paper had its special correspondent, who fought and wrote about it, giving his own version of matters." Predictably, the Kansas "news" combined a "total disregard of facts" with ringing contrasts of the noble, doughty "men of the North" with those skulking, vicious "minions of the Slave Power." "Tales of butchery, massacre, and murder, 'furnished by lying correspondents and telegraphic reporters, were going the rounds of the Northern abolition press' . . . 'falsehoods too palpable to be believed even by the vilest abolition fanatics,' yet their flow went on unchecked." Inspired, "poets praised in verse the deeds of the Free State cause"; artists turned out blatantly propagandist "graphics" to be relentlessly reproduced. World opinion—and "history"—were being coldbloodedly molded into a "South-bashing" form, never to cease to this day.

Winning all the pitched battles, the South was losing a war of whose existence she was hardly even aware. She was the victim of her virtue—though moderns disparage the supposed Southern "fear of abstraction" rather as a vice, a backwardness: "abstraction" meaning our own ever more hallucinatory reality of mere "media." Southerners—still hewing to the *code duello*—believed that words should match deeds. When Sumner slandered his uncle in the Senate, Preston Brooks forthrightly cracked a cane over his head. Tuttutting Northerners had learnt cunning. In a world of ever yellower journalism there just were no deeds, only words. Truth was not what happened but what the newspapers said—as Missouri was bitterly finding out in Kansas. She flashed her quixotic sword and cried "Come out and fight like a man!" and freesoilers pointed

19

and smirked "See the nasty old bully!" The Missouri Brookses broke heads; the Kansas Sumners broke heads too, but more importantly they called press conferences and flaunted their wounds.

At heart, then, it was a fight between clashing views of life, another battle in the "culture war," as it's now known—the ceaseless seesaw (as all Anglo-American history has been called) between Roundhead and Cavalier. ("Indeed, at many points," as Winston Churchill puts it, "the grim struggle . . . resembled and reproduced in its passions the antagonisms of the English Civil War.") The Missouri Cavaliers let their every human failing show: for aren't we all "only human"? Certainly not, retorted the "men of the North"! In the Civil War Kansas soldiers bragged that they eschewed tobacco and drink, read a chapter of the Bible every evening—and stole silverware and shot their prisoners. Here we confront the Puritan—politically the Radical—at his purest: the ideologue, Burkhardt's "terrible simplifier," untroubled by grotesque paradox, likely even blissfully unaware of it. Granted, the Missourians were shameful slackers all around—they drank, smoked, and slighted their Bible-reading, silver-stealing, and shooting of prisoners.

The overarching "terrible simplification" of the day came from the pen of James Redpath, the *New York Tribune* correspondent, a longtime professional agitator "so emotionally unstable that he could not make a straightforward statement of fact even when it would have been in his advantage to do so." Co-compiler of *Tales and Traditions of the Border* back in his native Scotland, Redpath branded the Missourians "Border Ruffians"; and his boss, the "controversial and erratic" Horace Greeley, took care that readers—of newspapers *and* history-books—knew all Missourians for "'Border Ruffians' and waiting secessionists," "'slaveocrats', whose only interest in Kansas was based on an unsavory and immoral hunger to expand slavery." This blanket vilification of a state, of a whole people, accelerated. The occupying Union army would behave accordingly in a few short years.

Outsiders still note the marked if subtle differences between Missouri and Kansas, laid down in these years; though often even Kansans and Missourians fall far short of understanding them. The Republicans' radical heritage and the Democrats' Southern, state-rights strain lie buried alike under the turnabouts and dumbings-down of twentieth-century politics; just as the numerical preponderance of liberal Methodists in the Kansas Border counties, as of conservative Baptists in the adjacent Missouri ones, lacks meaning in an age that dislikes or denies all such distinctions.

In Missouri, South-style, politics by tradition is the province of "lawyers and rich landowners"; in Kansas, rather, of "preachers, teachers, and small farmers, who put 'moral' and 'natural' rights first, legal and property rights second." Kansas, too, is a harsher place to live. "Far from markets, burned by drought, beaten by hail, withered by hot winds, frozen by blizzards, eaten out by grasshoppers"—and, at first, harried by Missourians—pioneer Kansans turned naturally to political extremes. "Abolitionism, Mormonism, Prohibitionism, Free Silver, the Nonpartisan League, Woman Suffrage"—all throve in Kansas. "Every incoherent and fantastic dream of social improvement and reform, every political fallacy," owns one Kansan, "rejected elsewhere, has here found tolerance and advocacy." The state's motto, *Ad Astra Per Aspera,* might be mischievously translated: "To the stars by the hardest possible ways!"

Missourians, by contrast, are seldom extremists. A friendlier environment and easygoing Southern culture unite to instill "a determination to cherish the old and consider skeptically the new." Here not geography rules, but history. "The state's mood and manner are a reminder of the sobering realities of history." Tricked, led astray by the tragic events of the 1850s and 60s, "Missouri was left with few illusions." She deserves her nickname, Paul C. Nagel implies: A long, tragic past "convinced many Missourians that 'you'll have to show me' was the most positive approach possible in the face of modern conditions." No utopian "To the stars!" for Missouri. Her motto, *Salus Populi Suprema Lex Esto*—most often given a demagogic twist—might more correctly be rendered, "Let the community wallow in its comfortable old ruts!"

The 1850s struggle was not, as commonly portrayed, merely a wicked Missouri assault on Kansas. "The conflict developed out of so complicated a course of events and over so long a period of time that it is futile to assume that there is such a thing as an initial aggressive act." Rather it was the first clash in the sectional war to come, with Kansas the prize. The struggle itself brought Kansas into being, molded the Kansas character—in violent opposition to Missouri's. Climate and demography took it from there. It was the plantation versus the sodhouse, with predictable results.

21

The fray groaned on through years of mutual recriminations, head-bashings, town-burnings, and "so-called elections" too wearying to recount. Before it was over, some two hundred people had been slain and $2 million in property destroyed—a staggering sum in a new, poor country. For the first couple of years the Missouri-dominated territorial legislature held sway, first from Shawnee Mission, comfortably close to the Border, then from proslavery Lecompton; Federal recognition—the implied support of Federal troops—afforded it the illusion of strength. The freesoilers, loudly bewailing their underdog role, bided their time, digging-in in the limitless hinterland, where they made Lawrence their Mecca, Topeka their secular, "outlaw"-government seat.

And time was on the "outlaw" side. The publicity being given the quarrel throughout the North was bringing in a tide of settlers, ever more spirited and meaner, that the South had no hope of matching. In the glare of near-universal condemnation cavalier Missouri hesitated—"Border Ruffians" agonized over their "image"! —and was lost. Late 1857 saw the freesoil faction moving inexorably toward power. The Southern presence in Kansas ebbed southeastward, the struggle itself soon to follow.

Southeast Kansas had changed less than other parts of the territory. Here Northerners had no easy entry by way of navigable rivers or friendly Iowa; while for Missourians from Kansas City south Kansas was only a walk or horseback ride away. Growing overland travel had caused "a wagon trail from Arkansas and country to the southeast" to be "developed by way of Fort Scott northwestward." Fort Scott itself, forsaken by the troops in 1853, had blossomed into a typical "Southern" town, complete with proslavery officials and newspaper. Some residents "had been driven from northern claims by freestate settlers," and daydreamed of revenge.

Freesoil firebrands eyed this final Southern bastion. James Montgomery, a fiery Campbellite, one of those countless preachers now preaching salvation through abolitionism, reserving hellfire only for slaveowners, made his home near Mound City, not far north of Fort Scott. In mid-May, 1858, for personal reasons, Montgomery declared a private war to drive out all Southern settlers in the Southeast. He soon had a Federal warrant on his head for horse-stealing and other less-than-idealistic deeds; but sympathetic army officers (such as Nathaniel Lyon, whom Missourians would soon know only too well) colluded to help him evade capture, and his campaign of lawlessness and violence went right on.

A leader among the embattled Southerners was Charles Hamilton—or Hamelton or Hambleton—rich, handsome scion of a fiery Georgia clan. His log mansion, rounded out by slave-quarters, lay three miles southeast of Trading Post, a small settlement on the Marais des Cygnes ("Marsh of the Swans," the upper Osage) River, hard by the old military road, just north of Fort Scott. The "Post" was quintessentially Southern—against abolition and temperance in equal measure. An "old-fashioned 'doggery' was in operation at the Post," and Montgomery, at the head of his private army, rode into town and "without ceremony proceeded to clean out the proslavery headquarters by emptying the contents of several barrels of sod-corn [=boiled corn] whiskey into the highway. Then he left a general notice to proslavery people to quit the territory."

Around the first of May, 1858, Montgomery descended on Hamilton's patrician bastion. Finding the building, built of logs and strengthened with palisades, too strong to be taken with small arms, Montgomery sent to Lawrence for a cannon, but before it arrived a bypassing body of Federal cavalry unsportingly broke up the siege. Hamilton, however, took the hint, sullenly "abandoned his claim and withdrew across the Border, resolved henceforth 'to vote and shoot in Kansas but for safety to sleep in Missouri'."

On May 19, thirteen Southern settlers lately driven from their claims vengefully rode back, an aroused Hamilton at their head. Seventeen sympathizing Missourians tagged along.

Afterwards, Hamilton told Missouri newspapers of a gunfight, fair and square. But the story flashed across the North and enshrined in Kansas mythology and in history-books was that these Border Ruffians, working from a list drawn up in advance, methodically rounded up eleven freesoil men in and around Trading Post, lined them up in a wooded ravine a bare quarter-mile west of the Border, mowed them down with rifle-fire, and finished them off—they thought—with revolvers. Five were killed, five badly wounded, though all lived, and one missed entirely. Desperately the living feigned death. Once the murder squad straggled off, the unhurt man rushed for help and started the news on its way.

The North stood appalled. The abolitionist machine cranked into high gear. Not four months later *Atlantic Monthly* published "Le

Marais du Cygne" by John Greenleaf Whittier, the "poet laureate of Abolitionism," "notorious for letting his indignation fly without bothering to consult the facts." Predictably, he got all of it wrong but the propaganda. His "reeds of the Swan's Marsh" were far away—deep in Missouri. Even the river to which the name had been misapplied wasn't very close. The Marais des Cygnes Massacre, as we call it, took place on a hillside, far from marshes and swans.

But no matter. The Border Ruffians—those "wolves of the Border," as Whittier has it—in the world's eyes had struck their worst, as well as their last; for now, finally, they were to be bearded in their den. The Battle of Kansas, to coin a Churchillian antithesis, was over; the Battle of Missouri was about to begin.

**THE MARAIS DES CYGNES MASSACRE**

24

# THREE
## *Jayhawkers*

For seven years before the Civil War broke out nationwide, war raged along the Border. Missouri gangs ranged Kansas almost unopposed during the first half of the period. Increasingly from 1857 on, Kansans brought the fight home to Missouri. Kansas outlaws, as the "law-and-order" *Leavenworth Herald* put it, "after stealing everything they can in Kansas . . . have extended their operations in the border counties of southwest Missouri." "The Jayhawkers," a historian concurs, "began, along about 1858, to raid and harrow the border counties of Cass, Bates, and Vernon. . . ."

A *Jayhawker* was one who behaved like a *jayhawk:* either the shrike or butcherbird or the common bluejay, with its "well-known disposition for breaking up the nests of other birds, taking things that don't belong to it, robbing the weak, and for constantly quarreling and fighting, with its incessant screeching and yelling." According to the *Oxford English Dictionary* a jayhawker "combined pillage with irregular warfare"; to jayhawk was "to raid."

The Missourians had invaded Kansas for a political end; the Kansans came to Missouri for plunder, and to settle the score. The Missourians had been led by their "establishment," their gentry; the

25

Kansan leaders were upstarts—"dregs of society" indeed, brought to the top by the turmoil of the times. James H. Lane—"an evil-looking creature with the sad, dim-eyed, bad-toothed face of a harlot"—by dint of Hitlerian persuasive powers had made himself Radical party-boss of Kansas. "A cynical, unscrupulous demagogue, Lane used without the least hesitation any and every kind of chicanery and skulduggery to gain his political and personal ends." Once he fled to Nebraska under indictment for horse-stealing. He would end up insane and a suicide. Equally feared and more respected by Missourians was Mound Citian James Montgomery, "whose name was more frequently in the mouths of Vernon County people from 1857 to 1862 than that of any other man." "His eye had the uneasy glare peculiar to haunted men, and his hollow laugh aroused the constant and unpleasant suggestion of a mind diseased." Another Mound Citian, Charles R. "Doc" Jennison, at first followed Montgomery's lead, but soon outgrew the older man's "strict moral sense" and acquired his own following, to whom the name Jayhawkers was first applied. Even to Montgomery he was "an unmitigated liar, black-leg, and robber." "His main contribution to the border troubles was his announced intention to make war against Missouri 'self-sustaining' . . . it meant simply that when he led a foray into Missouri, his followers were not only permitted, but encouraged, to pillage to their hearts' content and to destroy what they could not carry away." His name "became a terror in Vernon and Bates counties in Missouri." Alliteratively "he became Jennison the Jayhawker." In the Civil War the Seventh Kansas Cavalry, which he was commissioned to raise and lead (one company was made up almost wholly of criminals and captained by an ex-convict) enjoyed the nickname Jennison's Jayhawkers. "No other regiment in the Union army," their biographer concedes, "had so bad a reputation." For his war services Jennison would be courtmartialed.

In lists of infamous Jayhawkers, John Brown seldom figures. His faraway "martyrdom" casts a convenient veil over his Kansas doings; and the best scholars discount his importance in any case. "He and his followers brought tragedy to innocent settlers in the southeastern part of the territory, but at most that was only a subordinate factor in the stream of events when taken as a whole."

And yet, of all the controversial characters of the stripe, Kansas comes closer to claiming him as a folk-hero than any other. As a wild-eyed, rifle-toting Moses, he dominates a wall of the Capitol in Topeka, courtesy of John Steuart Curry; Osawatomie honors him in bronze, Kansas City in granite. Bewhiskered sculptures and mural alike are myths literally to a hair; the man of flesh was cleanshaven throughout his Kansas career, as period tintypes prove.

An aging, restless ne-er-do-well, abrim with muddled abolitionist zeal—"a crazy man for years," according to old acquaintances— Old Brown followed the younger Browns to the Osawatomie area in 1856, and in the troubled Kansas waters at last found his element. Incendiary doings of other Browns were credited to him. With his sons and others he rushed to the defense of Lawrence against the Missourians, and as the oldster in the crowd was dubbed captain of their extralegal "militia." On the strength of this two-day "commission" he was forever after "Captain Brown." "Under the circumstances the choice of a commander of so casual and temporary a unit possessed little or no significance." Far from "captaining" the town's defenses, Brown left in a huff because the real leaders wouldn't follow his harebrained advice; Brown, points out James Malin, was "incompetent to manage anything."

To vent his frustration and reassert his leadership at least over his own sons, Brown led four of the sons, a son-in-law, and two others aside from the homecoming Osawatomie crew. That night they dragged five poor-white Southern settlers out of their cabins along Potawatomie Creek. Their bodies were found next day, cutlass-hacked and decapitated. A Brown worshipper would call this "the execution of the leaders of the Lawrence raid"! But to Kansans the truth was instant and common knowledge: The killers were recognized from desciptions, and Brown was seen next day riding a horse known to have belonged to one of the victims. In the territorial district court indictments for murder and other crimes were handed down and warrants issued. But lawmen had trouble finding the suspects; Brown himself had prudently fled back East, fudging or denying all. Within two years the territorial and county governments had passed into freesoil hands. In 1859 the legislature repealed all its predecessor's laws, and no provision was made for continuance of prosecutions already underway. The Potawatomie Massacre, as it was called—which really "precipitated the conflict in southeastern Kansas," a region hitherto relatively free of political strife—was righteously swept under the rug.

Brown's aspirations, along with his notoriety, outgrew Kansas. He'd long cherished the dream of ending slavery in one fell swoop, touching off a black uprising by means of a raid into the heart of the South through the Appalachians. But his backers—wealthy, influential Eastern idealists who reveled in bankrolling mayhem in faraway Kansas in a good cause—boggled at treason nearer home. On the strength of his new cutlass-carved renown, Brown toured the East for two years doggedly peddling them his scheme and half-baking his plans. Then his English "military adviser," put off by Brown's erraticalness and slow pay, "deserted" and leaked details. The "Secret Six"—Brown's key backers—suffered assorted attacks of nerves and decreed indefinite postponement. Go back West, they implored; lie low till the heat dies down.

And so the summer of 1858 found a frustrated Brown back in Kansas—a now "deplorably quiet" Kansas—by no means planning to lie low but rather resolved to pull off some smallscale, western version of his raid to prove it could be done. The Secret Six were not deceived. Dispassionately they speculated about it to each other in their letters. Look for "an insurrection on the Kansas border" or "in some inland part of Missouri," wrote sanctimonious schoolmaster-editor Franklin B. Sanborn, "some mysterious 'Union-splitting' operation on the Missouri border." For the first time, if hardly the last, quiet, respectable intellectuals, including Christian ministers, were underwriting violence and terrorism in a "noble" cause. Not one of them thought to warn the endangered Missourians.

Brown, aliased "Shubel Morgan," settled down miles east of his old haunts, where he was rather too well-known, on the very site of the Marais des Cygnes Massacre. Not a hundred yards from the fatal ravine he built "Fort Snyder," named for his crony, landowner Eli Snyder, a stout walnut or pecan log cabin or blockhouse, located "right on a conspicuous place, in full view for miles around in Missouri." (Timbered today, the "conspicuous place" was then totally bare.) Around him gathered a bizarre, paramilitary menagerie: wildeyed young idealists, fugitives from justice, sticky-fingered old Kansas hands, European anarchists lacking only sputtering bombs, even a minor English poet. The captain's rules called for "division of the proceeds from the sale of loot much after the fashion of Caribbean pirates." As became a pirate chief and soon-to-be fugitive, Brown began raising the famous beard.

On Sunday, December 19, 1858, Brown stalwart George B. Gill, out scouting, crossed paths with a Missouri slave named Jim, "a fine-looking mulatto," seemingly engaged in peddling brooms. Gill took him along to see Brown, then at "Bain's Fort," another freesoil stronghold some seven miles deeper into Kansas on the Little Osage River. Jim got home very late that night—detained, he swore (if not to his wife), by the charms of an Osage squaw.

The following night, two dozen men—six more than would make the immortal raid on Harpers Ferry less than a year later—in two columns, packing "a miniature arsenal," set out from Fort Snyder, over into slumbering, unsuspecting, wintry Missouri.

The main file of fifteen men was led by Brown himself. Southeast they rode, along the chain of low, timbered "mounds" or ridges here paralleling the Border, toward the "plantation" of Jim's prosperous master—his *late* master, for James Lawrence had died in his bed back on February 28; his property was in probate and in the care of his son-in-law, Harvey G. Hicklin, Henry Township constable, who was living in the house with his wife and children.

When the raiders rumbled into the yard and demanded entry, Hicklin just had time to spring from bed and hide his money before the door burst in. While the intruders were turning the place upside down, helping themselves to saddles, boots, shotguns, and other choice articles, Brown himself strolled in and affably told the night-shirted Missourian not to be alarmed, they were merely "doing the Lord's will." The Lord, it seemed, willed them to pillage the farmstead of its livestock, wagons, provisions, and equipment—and incidentally its five black slaves: a "boy" named Sam; the broom-peddling Jim; Jim's wife Narcissa; and their two small children. Moving along to the nearby LaRue farm, Brown picked up five more slaves —"also six head of good horses, one wagon, 800 pounds of pork, a lot of bedding, clothing and many other articles." Retreating, they took along two white men as temporary hostages.

The remaining nine raiders, meanwhile, swooped down on the house of David Cruise, farther south across the Little Osage River. One account puts this column under the leadership of Aaron D. Stevens; other sources award the honor to John Henry Kagi, "an articulate and highly intelligent young schoolteacher," a *New York Post* reporter, and a longtime radical activist who'd once castrated a proslavery Kansas judge with a lucky (!) revolver shot. Acquaintances called him "a melancholy brigand," a religious skeptic, clever with words. Brown relied on him heavily, and he'd ridden on many a foray with Montgomery, including one only four days before on Fort Scott (boycotted by Brown when Montgomery wouldn't agree to burn the whole town) during which he combined the roles of participant and "objective" reporter by helping kill Deputy U. S. Marshal J. H. Little and then himself penning the New York newspaper account of the event! In Brown's revolutionary "provisional government" for the post-slavery U. S. set up in Canada earlier in the year, Kagi had been named "secretary of war." He would meet his bloody end on the river bank at Harpers Ferry.

Cruise, a modestly substantial farmer, though he owned only two slaves, doubtless was targeted simply because of his prosperity—his reputation for "buried gold." He was an old man, but also a man of spirit. As neighbors told it, when the raiders banged on the door, filling the night with threats and curses, Cruise leaped out of bed and caught up his revolver; but the cylinder became entangled in a ribbon, would not revolve, and so could not be fired. As Cruise threw down the useless weapon, the door gave way and one of the men outside fired. Cruise "fell near the fireplace and died almost instantly, his blood flowing out upon the hearth-stone."

Yet, according to Cruise's young son Rufus, writing many years afterwards, the raiders gained entry by subterfuge, pretending to be travelers seeking a night's shelter. Taking pity on them, Cruise called off his dogs and opened the door. Inside, the men gathered around the fire; then suddenly one of them drew his pistol. "I broke out of the house on the porch," Rufus wrote, "and I heard the pistol shot that killed father. I am sure it was Al Hazlitt shot him." Nightclothed and barefoot, the boy fled over frozen ground covered with six inches of snow, three miles to a kinsman's home.

"The 'liberators', in their heroic efforts in aid of the cause of freedom, now began a systematic pillage of the entire premises." "In an upstairs bedroom, one held a gun to Mrs. Cruise's head, forcing her to open all the closets. Then the band left, taking Cruise's horses, a wagon laden with provisions, two yoke of oxen, jewelry, and one female slave. When they rejoined Captain Brown and the others Hazlett [sic] was riding a fine new horse."

When the raiders first came, wrote Rufus, their "middleaged" slave woman, Jane, saw them through the window, knew their real purpose, and laughed. "She went back to the kitchen and began to pack up." "She took with her $60 in money, part hers and part my mother's." According to the county history, "She was unable to escape [the raiders]; perhaps she was unwilling but at any rate she was unable. A few days later she gave birth to a child."

Cruise's other slave, "a likely man named George," according to Rufus, was away "sparking" a slave woman at the nearby Martin home. In the neighbors' version he was at home but "fled in terror" and hid from his would-be liberators. In any case he returned home afterwards and remained with his murdered master's family.

"Father's pants were on a chair by the bed," Rufus added, "and the robbers took $30 in gold out of the pockets." They missed the "buried gold," though—buried in the saddle-shed, said Rufus.

Cruise's killer's identity has been much mooted. Neighbors blamed Bill Beckford, a personal enemy of Cruise's who knew the country and guided the raiders to the house. Yet, following the abortive Harpers Ferry raid some ten months later, the fatally wounded Aaron Stevens confessed that *he* had fired the shot that killed Cruise, that cold night back in faraway Vernon County, Missouri. "A tall, dark-haired young man with a rich voice and commanding presence who called himself Captain Charles Whipple," Stevens had met Brown in 1856, when he was "already known as a Free-State raider; it was less well known that he had deserted from the United States army after murdering an officer."

Stevens' guilt was confirmed by Jane, Cruise's ex-slave. During their epic journey north, Jane struck up a romance with Sam Harper, the Lawrence slave "boy," and after their arrival in Canada they married. Interviewed there in 1895 by historian Wilbur H. Siebert, Jane declared "her master would certainly have fired upon the intruders had not Whipple [Stevens] fired first, with deadly effect"—a startling moral equating of the intruder's right to murder his host with the householder's right of self-defense!

Yet Rufus Cruise firmly blamed Hazlitt; and an eyewitness's account would seem convincing. But 13-year-old Rufus was not really an eyewitness; he was already out on the porch when the shot was fired. Nor could he have been too clearheaded under the circumstances. And it seems strange that Stevens, on his deathbed, would confess to a murder he hadn't done. Legally, of course, it made no difference—the raiders were all equally guilty.

31

Leaving Cruise's, Kagi and crew next called on Hugh Martin, who lived half a mile east. Since he wasn't a slaveowner at all they were able to liberate from him only a "valuable mule." The sluggish rays of the December dawn here cut the liberatings short.

As the Border slowly awoke to the night's events, Brown paused—not at Trading Post as he claimed but in Augustus Wattles's house in Moneka, not far north of Mound City—to issue a "press-release," his so-called "Parallels," sent to Greeley's *New York Tribune,* as well as to Kansas newspapers, wherein "he weirdly distorted the facts of his raid." The mulatto Jim, he said, had sought him out with a woeful tale of suffering in bondage and a plea for rescue. His dead master's slaves were about to be "sold down the river" to Texas, that bogey-land of brutish toil, lethal climate, and fiendish masters. What could a humanitarian do but ride blindly to the rescue? Murder and grand larceny—never mind.

Modern interest, inevitably, centers on Sam and Jane, the two slaves between whom love seemingly blossomed on the long trek to freedom. Some of the romance fades, however, when we recall that "middleaged" Jane was pregnant, most likely by Cruise's "George," and gave birth on one of the first days in Kansas, and that the Lawrence estate's appraisers described Sam as "one Negro boy, supposed to be about 18 years old." Their respective ages are impossible to tell in Siebert's 1895 photograph.

Escorted by Brown and his chief henchmen, the fugitive party skirted the Missouri Border, crossed southern Iowa in the dead of winter, and continued on to Chicago by rail, "in a stock car." There the detective Allan Pinkerton, then an abolitionist activist, took charge. On March 12, 1859—2,400 hard miles from Missouri—they were "ferried across the Detroit River" to "Canada West" (Ontario), where some of their descendants live to this day.

"The Northern press made the Missouri incursion a heroic rescue of slaves against great odds." And Northerners, as was becoming their habit, believed what they read in the papers, even against prior inclination. Sympathy for the slaves easily became applause for their "liberator" and his good works. Had he really done them a favor, though? "It is difficult to conceive a more heart-rending experience," writes Dwight L. Dumond, "than leaving in perpetuity one's native soil, relatives, friends, and occupation, whether it is done voluntarily or by compulsion." Surely sudden,

32

forcible "liberation" constituted "a greater cruelty than enslaving their ancestors in the beginning." Literally, of course, as John Brown bragged, "eleven persons are forcibly restored to their natural and inalienable rights," and by 1895 the ex-slaves defended the deed. It was all too easy to discount the murder of one who "fought against the liberation"—i.e. of his worldly goods! It was all too easy to spare no sympathy for widowed Lucinda Cruise. Southern denunciations of the raid as the doings of criminals or madmen were drowned in abolitionist exultations and journalistic irresponsibility.

"When the news of the invasion of Missouri spread," wrote Redpath, "a wild panic went with it which in a few days resulted in clearing Bates and Vernon counties of their slaves." Borderers, however, seemed strangely unaware of their panic. Indeed, the Border itself bore little resemblance to the place being described by Redpath and his ilk. Slavery loomed ludicrously small in the local economy and consciousness. Slaves—only 2.8 percent of the population, a marked decline since 1850—lived and worked alongside their masters. "Planter" David Cruise was a sturdy, hard-working yeoman farmer—the type of whom Northerners affected to be so fond. James Lawrence was a Border rich man—with his 160-acre "plantation" and his five slaves, two of them babes in arms! The neighborhood knew no "Border Ruffians."

Certainly its reaction bespoke innocence of anything but hurt pride. "The second day, about 250 men . . . hovered about the Kansas line a while, but at last sneaked back home." Grown scrupulous and defensive about their cause, Borderers decided to show the world just how law-abiding they were—leaving it to Federal troops in Kansas to make the sole attempt to take Brown by force, an effort thwarted by lawbreaking freesoilers who went to Brown's rescue in the so-called "Battle of the Spurs."

The day after the raid, Harvey Hicklin and Isaac LaRue went before Justice of the Peace N. R. Marchbanks and swore that they'd been robbed, of such-and-such, by so-and-so—"and further deponent says not." A petition signed by all local leaders, beseeching state protection from outlaw Kansas, accompanied copies of the affidavits to Jefferson City. Governor "Bob Stewart drunk," having managed to become "Bob Stewart sober," repeatedly urged the General Assembly to act—since he believed only legislative action could constitutionally address the issue. But not till February 24,

1859, did the solons essay even a feeble first step. And the feckless Buchanan administration in Washington sent its condolences. Legends to the contrary, neither state nor nation put a price on John Brown's head. The bloodied Border was on its own.

It did its best. Next May, during the regular circuit court session in Nevada, a grand jury of prominent Vernon Countians found true bills of indictment against John Brown and all his men, known and unknown, for grand larceny and murder. But Brown, who was fast attaining sainthood in many Northern eyes, could now thumb his nose at slave-state warrants. It was left to Virginia to do the judicial honors after the crime had been more famously if less successfully repeated at Harpers Ferry, ten months later.

Northerners were to become mighty sticklers for law in a couple of years. Meanwhile many had gone in for "higher law." Flimsy enough in itself, the "higher law" in this case took off on a tissue of lies. Apart from Brown's claim that Jim—"a most astonishing liar"—*said* so, nothing suggests that the Lawrence slaves either had been mistreated or were about to be sold. Lawrence's great-granddaughter Bessie Carlton, told the story, shook her head firmly. A researcher, sifting the copious Lawrence probate papers, agreed Brown's case is shaky: "In view of the will of James Lawrence I find this difficult to believe." And generally pro-Union historian Allan Nevins magisterially sums up, "The sale was a fiction." Either Jim deceived John Brown or John Brown deceives us.

Clearly Brown's defenders are deceived by his oft-echoed references to the "estate" to which the slaves belonged. In abolitionist fantasies this took on the aspect of a vast landed property over which some Simon Legree duly cracked his whip. In fact it was an estate simply *in law*—a dead man's worldly goods.

Lawrence had willed that the slaves be hired out until his youngest child came of age. To have sold them sooner would have breached sacrosanct laws; and in fact the estate wasn't settled till 1866. Meantime the administrator, widely respected neighborhood pioneer Peter Duncan, planned simply to take the slaves up to Jackson or Lafayette counties and there hire them out to hemp-planters. Bad-apple Jim—a veteran of "the hemp-breaks of Jackson," spied his chance; and in Jim's tall tale John Brown saw his: "a 'heaven-sent' opportunity" to wreak a sensation in the national press and win support for his major, Eastern raid.

The Border, moreover, knew the idealistic heroes of this Northern newspaper-epic for what they really were: not just Brown himself as the indicted butcher of Potawatomie Creek but many of the others as notorious frontier characters—human vultures long-ranging over "Bleeding Kansas" fattening on proslavery or freesoil carcasses with marvelous impartiality. They rode along that cold night either for personal gain or to settle personal scores. One of the first into the Lawrence house was James Steele, who knew the place well enough to rush straight to Hicklin's money-drawer. The raiders of Cruise's were led there by Bill Beckford, a "desperate character" who "knew the country well and hated Cruise personally." Rufus Cruise, who fingered Albert Hazlitt for his father's murder, knew the "mean-looking" Kansas desperado by sight. His mother, he said, knew five of the nine "liberators."

The goods and money taken with the slaves. Brown declared—theirs anyhow according to the Marxist labor theory—were needed for their immediate care. Yet just days later, his own eulogists tell us, "the Abolitionists of Franklin County, Kansas, were supplying the Negroes with food and clothing, 'of which they were greatly in need'." And a sympathetic Iowan was soon calling them "the saddest specimens of humanity I have ever seen." Beckford, Hazlitt, Steele, et al, it must be assumed, were then busily trying on Harvey Hicklin's boots and overcoats and jubilantly jingling David Cruise's golden eagles in their pockets. And their sterling "captain" shortly was in Cleveland "publicly selling the 'liberated' Missouri horses that had hauled the party east" and sending the money to his family. "A genuine participation in the whole matter of 1776," a latterday admirer sums up—truly a novel twist to the Spirit of '76!

"Do you hear the news from Kansas?" enthused Gerrit Smith, one of the Secret Six, reputedly the richest man in America. "Our dear John Brown is invading Missouri and pursuing [there] the policy which he intended to pursue elsewhere [i.e. slave-raiding the South]." "The name of John Brown soared aloft—and the name of David Cruise," "the old gray-headed pioneer . . . guilty of no offense whatever," "vanished beneath the notice of idealists."

"[Brown's] principles were those of Russian Nihilists, who would destroy the present and see what the future would bring." Far from being justified by previous violence, his actions really "precipitated the conflict in southeastern Kansas." High among the

35

Kansas crimes, concludes James Malin, "were lying and hate and the intimidation of truth—all in the name of humanitarian idealism."

To give Brown's grubby, hate-breeding deed—"a typical Jayhawker foray," "an indefensibly lawless outrage upon inoffensive citizens"—lofty idealistic significance is to ignore its jayhawking essence and Jayhawker context. It was the eighth major raid on Missouri in liberty's name, and hardly the last. Just ten days later a dozen Jayhawkers under Brown's crony Eli Snider attacked and burned Jeremiah Jackson's store on the Border in Bates County. "Despite efforts by the Federal authorities to suppress them, the jayhawkers continued to ride amuck throughout 1859 and 1860." The latter year brought a campaign of lynchings and shootings of moderates throughout southeastern Kansas in revenge for vigilante hangings of Jayhawker horsethieves. On November 12 Jennison visited Trading Post to finish Montgomery's good work begun there two years before; two men were lynched, including Samuel Scott, a Missourian chosen to be Vernon County's first sheriff. "In the name of freedom in Kansas," growled a Missourian, "great freedom was taken with other people's lives and property."

Montgomery himself threatened to invade Fort Scott, again, to prevent the Federal court from hearing cases against himself and his followers, and to prevent the Federal land sales scheduled for December 5, which they felt would benefit proslavery men.

The threat alone panicked the whole area. The judge and the last Southern settlers fled into Missouri, spreading word of coming invasion. The state militia at last was called out; the so-called Southwest Expedition manned the Border in Vernon County.

It was both too late and too soon. The Border War was lost, the Civil War itself not yet begun. Kansans could now afford to wait. Great days were dawning—the Republican party had swept Washington, the South was leaving the Union. Jayhawking was turning respectable—nay, patriotic!

# FOUR
## *The Twelfth Star*

Recent years have seen both growing popular interest in the War Between The States (officially so-called in Resolutions of Congress) and, it seems, diminishing popular understanding of it. And no aspect is more poorly understood—even by Missourians—than the part played in the war by "this unhappiest of states."

Almost everything that can be said of "Civil War" Missouri (where it was a *civil* war indeed: internecine, brother-against-brother) rings wrong. Missouri a superstate, the "Giant of the West," economically the largest slave state? Missouri—backwater Missouri, far from the famous battlefields—the cockpit of the bitterest fighting, the nakedest struggle over the issues, the worst injustices, the terriblest trashing of revered American values? Missouri, "loyal" Missouri, attacked by the Federal army, more brutally occupied than any foreign land? Missouri, which in schoolbooks never seceded, the twelfth star in the Confederate Battle Flag?

Since, according to finespun Federal theory, Missouri never left the Union, and for most of the war was under Federal occupation, with conscription ruthlessly in force, "officially" more Missourians served with the Union than the Confederate forces. *(Did* they, though? The statistics are suspect at best. Federal totals often include troops actually raised in other states, men who moved to Missouri during the war, and unwilling conscripts, many of them former—and still at heart—Rebels. And Confederate figures are hopelessly incomplete.) The myth of "loyal" Missouri and her "partnership" with the Union waxes ever stronger.

Missouri's position was unique literally from the ground up. First, she was "upside down," her Unionists in the south and east, her Southerners in the north and west—"Little Dixie." Ever more these prosperous conservatives, though fairly ruling state politics, were haunted by their own and the state's geographical exposure. It was this maddening sense of danger that had fueled their fight for Kansas—an effort that backfired, simply realizing their worst fears. Missouri's meddling in the Territory, as magnified in abolitionist propaganda, turned all the North against her. No other state fell into all-out war with so many readymade, virulent foes.

Not only was Missouri cut off from the Deep South; she was cut in two. The Missouri River, superbly navigable and still unbridged, formed the Federal lifeline to both the Pacific and the new Colorado goldfields. Missouri's flesh-and-blood, the South, could get along without her; the North, obliged to wage offensive, coast-to-coast war, could not. "Missouri had to be held for the Union."

The 1860 election betrayed Missourians' tortured consciousness of their unique plight. Southern extremists swept state offices; yet of the four presidential candidates Missouri supported moderate Democrat Stephen Douglas, well-meaning author of the tragic Kansas-Nebraska Act—it was a stunning comment on her political isolation that Douglas carried not one other state.

Then, lurching to the other pole, the voters in early 1861 brought together an ultraconservative Constitutional Convention charged to weigh Missouri's relationship to the Union in light of the deepening crisis brought on by the Southern states' secessions. The Convention turned out to be "from Missouri" indeed: Let others secede; skeptic old Missouri would wait to be "shown."

Alas—there were those more than eager to "show" her, burrowing busily in either wing. Governor Claiborne F. Jackson, fire-eating veteran of the Kansas battles, plotted secretly with Southern leaders to take Missouri into the Confederacy. In April he spurned Lincoln's call for volunteers to coerce the seceding South. "Your requisition . . . is illegal, unconstitutional and revolutionary in its objects, inhuman and diabolical, and cannot be complied with." At the same time, "rash, headstrong, and excitable" Unionist leaders, largely in St. Louis, coldbloodedly schemed to commit Missouri to the Federal cause even if it meant the violent overthrow of her government. Their leader, Frank P. Blair, Jr., raised and armed "Home Guards" among the St. Louis Germans.

He was ably seconded by Captain Nathaniel Lyon, a blunt, fanatical, puritanical abolitionist fresh from Kansas, where he'd learnt to hate Missourians. A striking psychological study, Lyon in fact "hated everybody." Like so many abolitionists, he'd forsaken the stern Calvinism of his New England forebears for a quirky private faith in salvation through social tinkerings. He confused his own ego with the will of God: Anyone who opposed him, therefore, was a devil, to be hounded from the face of the earth.

On May 10—spurning a compromise worked out by his commander, General William H. Harney, who chanced to be out of town—Lyon surrounded and forced the surrender of State Guardsmen assembled—lawfully, but in Lyon's eyes with designs on the Federal arsenal—in "Camp Jackson" in St. Louis. (A secessionist mob had just sacked the Liberty arsenal; yet Lyon himself had "sacked" the St. Louis site, sneaking the arms over to Illinois.) Marching the disarmed troopers through downtown St. Louis—"a deliberate act of provocation"—his undisciplined, hated German soldiers found themselves beset by angry citizens. Panicking, they fired into the crowd, killing 30 and wounding some 75—men, women, children. Next day six more were slain.

"Brief and distorted accounts" of the event in Eastern papers gave instant birth to the myth of "Lyon as a hero whose resolute action had saved the state." In fact he did both his own cause and the state grave harm. Lyon may have "saved" Missouri, scholars agree, but "only in a feverishly diseased condition . . . certain to grow worse." "From this moment Missouri was given over to four years of violence." "And more than any other single individual, Nathaniel Lyon bore responsibility for this fratricidal tragedy."

"News of the 'Camp Jackson Massacre' aroused fierce excitement throughout Missouri and produced a strong reaction in favor of the pro-Confederate party." "If Unionism means such atrocious deeds," said an erstwhile staunch Unionist, "I am no longer a Union man." Tardily the General Assembly voted a Military Bill—branded by the Federals "an indirect secession ordinance." General Sterling Price, Mexican War hero and moderate-Unionist Convention president, was appointed commander of the State Guard, the independent Missouri army. Governor Jackson had his fight—or rather Lyon had his, for the fire-eating governor felt a last-minute blush of Missouri caution. On June 11 he and Price went to St. Louis under a safe-conduct and parleyed with Lyon and Blair at the Planter's House in a last-minute try for a compromise peace.

Rewarded for his massacre by being promoted four grades at once to brigadier general and given Harney's job by peace-loving President Lincoln, Lyon wrecked the conference by his intransigence. When the Missourians began proposing certain restraints to be exercised by both sides, Lyon cut them off: "Better the blood of every man, woman, and child within the limits of the State should flow, than that she should defy the federal government." (A typical ideologue, living in a world of abstractions, he'd no time for mere human beings—indeed, he literally hated most of them. And his call for blood would be abundantly filled.) Missouri mustn't just stay in the Union, as he saw it, she must actively support it. "Either submission or resistance to the federal government," that was the choice. It was a revolutionary reinterpretation of the state-federal relationship, as a dismayed governor tried to point out.

"This means war," Lyon sneered, and stalked from the room. Jackson and Price shook off their stunned silence and raced back to Jefferson City, burning their bridges behind them, figuratively and literally alike. A jumped-up captain of infantry had declared war on a state of the Union, still innocent of any disloyal act!

It was only the beginning. On June 15, Lyon's army occupied the Missouri capital, hard on the fleeing state government's heels. Two days later, at Boonville, it routed a green rearguard of state troops. On July 20, overshadowed by Federal bayonets, a reconvened rump of the Convention dutifully, and with flagrant illegality, *declared the state legislature abolished and the offices of governor and other elected officials vacant* and filled them from its own ranks, in effect seeking to govern the state itself. By October, almost half the original members of the Convention had been arrested for "treason." Shades of "Pride's Purge" and the revolutionary Long Parliament! Victor-written postwar histories make much of the "cooperation" between Convention-run Missouri and the Union (as expressed in 1162 battles and skirmishes?); but why not? It was Vichy "cooperating" with Berlin. The Convention—the Union's puppet—was a revolutionary council, not a government, and the Union would treat it with a deserved contempt.

The legal government, meanwhile—the one the people had elected—was setting an example for certain regimes in World War II. In October Governor Jackson called the General Assembly into session at Neosho, on the lower Border, and this body duly enacted an Ordinance of Secession. Standard, "victor history" either ignores the action altogether or ridicules it, implying that the Convention alone had the power to secede—though surely the body that had granted that power in the first place had the power to take it back again; and the Union grudged other secessions by legislatures. Unionists are also quick to point out that (minus dubious proxies) the two houses fell far short of quorums—fudging the fact that the Convention fell even shorter! The verdict remains "not proven either way." Granted secession under such irregular conditions was desperate at best; but it was desperation all around, hardly the moment for proper form; and might would make right in any case. The invading "army of freedom" was seeing to that.

Missouri, then, had *two* governments (actually *three;* martial law, declared on August 20, 1861, made the Federal military command the *real* government): one propped up by Federal arms and staffed by "scalawags," figures from the shadows who in saner days had been unable to break into politics on their merits; the other duly elected but driven from its seat. Sent to Richmond, its delegates were recognized on November 20 and formally seated in the Confederate Congress; and the Southern Battle Flag added its twelfth star. (Its thirteenth, Kentucky, would also remain unacknowledged by the North.) After weary months in fleeing carriages and dreary Arkansas hostelries, the government-in-exile of "occupied Missouri" settled down for the duration at Marshall, Texas. When Governor Jackson died—in bed—late in 1862, urbane but difficult Lieutenant Governor Thomas C. Reynolds took his place, to carry on to the bitter end, as well as circumstances would permit.

Yes, circumstances were pinched. Lyon's kill-or-cure measures had had their effects. Missouri's native conservatism surfaced, waverers wavered worse. Many who might have joined Jackson and Price in Jefferson City shrank from joining them as fugitives of dubious future. The Boonville skirmish had assured the Federals control of the Missouri River west to the Border, as well as all the northern half of the state, and left them positioned to strike south from river and railheads virtually as and where they would.

The Border, meantime, had watched these events with mixed concern and exhilaration. Once more, geography told. Hill countians—like mountaineers always—felt sheltered from the quarrel, able to remain neutral or even lukewarmly Unionist. Western Missourians—like all flat borderlanders—*had* to take sides. For them, moreover, the news from St. Louis and Jefferson City only reinforced the strong feelings forged in the Kansas fight. "For some time an open warfare had been waged with the Kansans and the prospect of a big fight, upon a concerted plan, did not terrify those accustomed to desultory 'scrimmages'." Southern Democrat Breckinridge had swept the Border; secessionist sentiment was actually stronger there even than in Little Dixie. On the Border recruitment of the State Guard was a gala community event.

Vernon County—a "miniature South Carolina"—was typical. "After Camp Jackson nineteen-twentieths of the people . . . favored the Southern cause." Abe Lincoln had gotten not a local vote; one old fellow wanted to vote for him but was chided out of such perversity! In nextdoor Bates County the few who voted for him "found their names posted at various public places . . . with a broad invitation that they might be happier elsewhere."

"Secession flags fluttered in the breezes"; ladies sewed secession banners and uniforms; speakers harangued, urging the people to "arm to the teeth and fight to the death against the black Abolitionists and the tyrannical Lincoln government."

"On the 12th of June came the call to arms" to units "substantially the same as those raised the previous winter" for the Southwest Expedition. On July 1 Governor Jackson himself spent a night at Montevallo on his flight south, even as the Vernon Countians hurried to join him and Price and other mustering State Guardsmen at Cowskin Prairie in the state's extreme southwest corner. Here, following the morale-lifting minor victory at Carthage, in which they "first smelled powder," the reported 483 Vernon County men became the core of the Seventh Cavalry Regiment of the Eighth Division, with Nevada's DeWitt Clinton Hunter, first and incumbent county and circuit clerk, elected as its colonel. According to report, proportionate to population, "Vernon County furnished more men for the rebel army" than any other in Missouri.

Southern fortunes in the state sprang back dramatically, if only temporarily, in the second half of 1861. Moving to seal his conquests by closing off the road to Arkansas—the Telegraph or Wire Road from Springfield southwest to Fort Smith—Lyon was lured on into fatal folly. His plan began unraveling when the raw Missourians routed Franz Sigel—a radical refugee from the failed 1848 German revolution—and the hated St. Louis "Dutch" at Carthage.

So far it was a war simply between the state of Missouri and the United States. The one hope for Jackson and Price lay in joining hands with the regular Confederates under Texas Ranger General Ben McCulloch in northern Arkansas. McCulloch was skeptical of the value of the green Missouri troops, as well as hesitant for tortuous political considerations. At last, by yielding top command, Price secured McCulloch's tactical cooperation. On August 9 his Texans and Louisianians entered Missouri and encamped along Wilson's Creek, fifteen miles southwest of Springfield, awaiting a break in the rain before attacking Lyon in the town.

Outnumbered, desperate—and disobeying orders—Lyon struck first. The battle—called "the Bull Run of the West"—seesawed fiercely all the following day. At last Lyon himself took a bullet through the heart; his demoralized forces streamed northeast in full retreat. The Missourians, much like the Confederates after Bull Run, found themselves too bloodied and wearied to pursue.

The summer, meantime, also had seen a revival of Border warfare. "The tocsin of war," conceded Governor Robinson of Kansas in after years, "was the signal for the resurrection of all the thieves, plunderers and murderers of territorial days." Or as John N. Edwards poetically puts it, "The forests were attacked by the plains." On July 18, the Jayhawkers—now baptized the Seventh Kansas Cavalry—pounced on unhostile, undefended Harrisonville. By the time a (Unionist) Missouri militia unit joined them the Kansans had broken into and robbed most of the stores. Included in the loot were the papers of the Cass County sheriff and much county money; mountains of county goods were packed into stolen wagons and sent to Kansas. Propserous, prominent Jackson County stockman Colonel Henry Younger—bearer of a name destined to be heard again—lost hundreds of thousands of dollars worth of horses, wagons, and carriages from his Harrisonville livery stable. Of Jennison's men Federal General Henry W. Halleck wrote, "They are no better than a band of robbers." Jennison's commissioning, he said, constituted "offering a premium for rascality and robbing generally." General James G. Blunt—himself no angel—would call another Kansas Unit, the Fifteenth, "the Forty Thieves."

And yet ever more their army was relying on such brigands. So far none of the Kansans had a commission—the governor *"would not* commission them because of their unsavory reputation, and President Lincoln *could not* make colonels of volunteers." Jim Lane was further disqualified by being a U. S. Senator, yet this didn't deter Lincoln from commissioning him a brigadier general. The regulars recognized and used the Kansas irregulars on the theory that "the enemies of our enemies are our friends"—and Missourians were now enemies one and all. The two sides in the old Kansas fight had traded places. Yesterday's fugitive horsethieves had turned into "patriots," even "generals." Yesterday's "law and order" folk were "rebels," damnable "traitors"—fair game for the righteous.

Lane, the overnight "general," set about gathering a private army, designed "to carry the old bloodstained banner of Kansas to the Gulf." Assured that cavalrymen "could each lead back a horse," and footsoldiers come back cavalry, "wild fellows flocked to his standard." This horsethieving "Army of Kansas" hovered around Fort Scott, now and then making riskless jayhawking forays. On August 20, part of Montgomery's troop bluffed a Missouri force from Balltown and burned the bridge and (Unionist-owned) mill.

Such news from home reached the Border soldiers in the aftermath of Wilson's Creek, where they were among the first Southerners engaged, though suffering few casualties. Reluctantly easygoing "Pap" Price let them go home to look after their families. McCulloch having gone back to Arkansas in a huff, Price himself followed north in a few days with his whole army of some 12,000, and camped near Nevada on the evening of August 31.

He sent out some 80 of his local men to spy out the Federals around Fort Scott. They broke up a Federal religious service (the Rev. Col. Montgomery himself was preaching) and drove back a mule herd. Next day, after skirmishing with Price's vanguard along Big Drywood Creek south of Deerfield, the Federals fled, leaving a panicked Fort Scott braced for attack. But political considerations forced Price to turn away from the Border and retake the heart of his own state. Held back at Big Drywood, the Missourians' energies brought stunning Southern victory at Lexington on September 20 after a fabled seven-day siege. "Rebel" spirits soared.

Lane, scorning his orders to support Union defense efforts along the Missouri, skulked along in Price's wake, chicken-stealing and town-burning. Passing through Butler, Bates County seat, Montgomery's men left a new church, the courthouse, and all the business buildings in ashes; Papinsville was treated likewise. On September 22 Lane reached Osceola, then one of western Missouri's major towns, crucial as the head of navigation on the Osage River and so as a military depot. It was also the home of Lane's own colleague, U.S. Senator Waldo P. Johnson. Nine civilians were "courtmartialed" and shot; all but three buildings were burned. After personally burning down the stately Johnson home and stealing the Missourian's fancy carriage, Lane called his cohort home toward Kansas, having destroyed or carried away in loot an estimated one

UNION SOLDIERS PILLAGING IN MISSOURI

45

million dollars worth of private property, including wagonloads of silk dresses and grand pianos. Atop the plunder 300 of his brave boys lay dead-drunk. Hundreds of stolen horses, mules, and slaves brought up the rear. Rev. Hugh Fisher, the "regimental chaplain," lugged stolen altar furnishings to equip his own unfurnished Kansas church. Northern observers called them "a ragged, half-armed, diseased, mutinous rabble, taking votes whether any troublesome or distasteful order should be obeyed or defied."

The Union was using sorry means to its lofty ends. On cushy "occupation duty" around Kansas City that fall Jennison's regiment jayhawked Parkville, Pleasant Hill, and Independence, and mixed grand larceny with Radical politics by forcibly freeing and arming slaves and openly auctioning Missouri loot in Kansas towns.

Independence, Harrisonville, Butler, Osceola—four Border county seats plundered and burned in the first months of the war; Jayhawkers riding unopposed "along the whole line of the border from the Kaw River to the Boston Mountains." It was a chilling foretaste of what was to come. For it was growing obvious that Price, despite his victories, could not quite break the Union grip on Missouri. He was plagued, like all early Civil War commanders, by the expiring short-term enlistments of many of his men. Nor were recruits swelling his ranks as readily as expected, or else were too raw for quick use. Sadly, Price pulled back from Little Dixie, his homeland, site of his late glorious triumph, high-water-mark of his fighting career and of Confederate fortunes in the West. Winter found the Missourians "settled down in rough camps on the Osage" around charred Osceola, while their commander worked on last-ditch measures to hold the Southwest and spread unrest and guerrilla war behind the lines in the rest of the state.

Price's successes, however, had forced the Federals to revise their own strategy, settling for humbler objectives. Conceding the Southwest for the time being, they would focus on holding the vital jugular of the Missouri-Mississippi, along the long oxbow-line Cape Girardeau-Rolla-Sedalia-Kansas City-the Border.

But they were reckoning without the guerrillas. As 1862 came, insurgent activity goaded them back onto the offensive. The new year, too, found them enjoying an ever-growing edge in numbers and equipment, and resolved to profit from the first year's blunders; while with his pinched resources Price could only pray the old strategy would work again. As in 1861, he withdrew south down the Wire Road, one jump ahead of the undistinguished new Union commander, Samuel R. Curtis, stretching out his lines of supply through the rugged, unfamiliar, unwelcoming Ozarks—and then turned on him together with the Confederate regulars.

But alas! this time the tables were turned. This time it was the Southerners who fled the field in disorder; this time it was *their* leaders lost to death or capture; Price himself suffered two painful flesh wounds. On March 6, 1862, around the Elkhorn Tavern on Pea Ridge, a few miles south of the Missouri line, stolid Curtis—aided and abetted by an obscure quartermaster captain named Phil Sheridan—spectacularly restored Union fortunes in the West.

Coupled with Confederate setbacks in the East, Pea Ridge had tremendous effects. Desperately the South needed reinforcements in Mississippi. Price forsook the state service for a Confederate commission, urging his officers and men to follow his example; and some 8,000 would do so all told. The only hope of a Missouri regained—*their* Missouri—was a Confederacy preserved.

But meantime, of course, Missouri was indeed given up as lost. Price quickly found himself caught up in byzantine Richmond intrigues—proposed as leader of the "Northwest Conspiracy," a wild scheme to break up the North, even as a replacement for Jefferson Davis. Price's men were fighting and dying at Corinth, Mississippi—if not restlessly melting away and slipping home.

At long last, in January, 1863, Price served notice on Richmond: Let them all be sent back west of the Mississippi, he warned, or he would follow his deserters' example—he, too, would desert to go back and "bushwhack it" in Missouri.

**CONFEDERATE BATTLE FLAG AND *MISSOURI* CONFEDERATE BATTLE FLAG**

# FIVE
## *Knights of the Bush*

There were bushwhackers—with a small *b*—decades before the War Between The States. The *Oxford English Dictionary* finds the word first used in print in Washington Irving's *Knickerbocker History* (1809): "They were gallant bush-whackers and hunters of raccoons by moonlight." The "bush" (German *bosch,* French *bois,* Spanish *bosque)* is, of course, the *forest.* A bushwhacker, then, is simply a backwoodsman, a Daniel Boone—"one accustomed to beat about or make his way through the bush."

By the spring of 1862, however, anyone making his way through the Missouri bush was apt to be a Confederate *guerrilla* ("little warrior," itself first borrowed from the Spanish by Wellington in the Napoleonic Wars). Unionist newspapers popularized the new definition of bushwhacking and gave it those unsavory overtones it still holds—since the winners of wars write the dictionaries as well as the history books ("one that fires from ambush," pontificates the feckless *Webster's Third;* "a deserter or draft dodger who became an outlaw"—contrast this with the *Oxford's* straightforward "a Confederate guerrilla"). Sarcastically the *Kansas City Journal* wrote of "Knights of the Bush"—of a "war of the roses and bushes." It wasn't the last time language would express the logical link between irregular warfare and wilderness. In World War II the partisans in occupied France were known as the *Maquis;* in French, *maquis* is originally a Corsican dialect word for "wild, bushy land."

The Border, be it remembered, was but the human or political form of the *timberline:* that ragged western edge of the mighty North American "bush." And it's illuminating to locate the Bushwhacker battlefields, famous or infamous, great and small—Lawrence, Fort Baxter, Centralia—in relation to the timberline or the Border. We find them strung along it like so many beads on a necklace. This was "border war" indeed. The country's marginal, "border" nature imposed itself on its people. White Borderers, like the Red ones before them, were coming to appreciate the Border's unique advantages as a setting for "little war." On the one hand there could be dramatic, long-range cavalry charges unhindered by natural obstacles; on the other the concealment, the "panther-stealth and hunting-cat seriousness of the forest fighting." Successful guerrilla warfare, concludes Clausewitz, needs a country "rough and inaccessible, because of mountains, forests, marshes," with a "scattered distribution of houses and farms."

"No region in America was better suited to guerrilla cavalry operations than western Missouri." "On the Kansas side," wrote a reporter, "the border is principally prairie, across which the eye can reach in all directions. When you enter Missouri, the face of it is entirely changed"; "the valleys are broken and densely wooded . . . places in which 5,000 men might hide, and an army march by the roads without knowing of their presence. . . ." "Broad belts of timber linked by large sweeps of prairie made the land ideal for sudden strikes and swift retreats." While hardly *causing* the "little war," the country made it possible and dictated its course.

What *did* cause it? Why should there be fierce guerrilla fighting in Missouri, fiercer than elsewhere? Why should even the state's premier soldier—rumored future Confederate president—speak seriously of giving up regular warfare in Mississippi for bushwhacking back in Missouri? Now that the battle-lines had moved far away, hadn't things at home begun to settle back toward normal? Well, that was what conservative Missourians had expected, why many of them had been willing to stand aside and let the likely winner finish the job as quickly—painlessly—as possible.

Their awakening was rude. As states'-rightists had long cautioned, the new Unionist principles were revolutionary—and revolutions are never quick or painless. Far from content simply with "saving the Union," proving Federal supremacy, the victors were doing in Missouri what they would afterwards do throughout the South: They were turning society upside down. By 1862, all over "occupied Missouri," the "natural leaders"—damned by their prewar support of "Southern" views—were being purged and replaced with creatures of the rump Convention, the self-styled "provisional government." The *real* government, meanwhile—the military one—was staking out powers nothing short of totalitarian.

Slain Lyon's worthy successor, John C. Fremont, the so-called Pathfinder, "was never able to find his way across the Missouri political terrain." His head lost in the clouds of Radicalism and self-importance, he instituted "a procedure of military surveillance, restriction, and coercion" in utter disregard of the provisional government, "as though Missouri were the ground of the enemy." He declared martial law in St. Louis on August 14, 1861, and six days later extended it throughout the state. (Lincoln himself extended it throughout the nation on Septener 20, 1862, by suspending habeas corpus, "and authorized the arrest of any person 'guilty of any disloyal practice,'" words that could be stretched to fit almost any case, a fact strangely overlooked in Lincoln hagiography.) Fremont's successors liked and retained his good works. For the first of them, Curtis, "'Rebel', 'guerrilla', and 'reptile' were synonyms."

On December 21, 1861, General Halleck promulgated the "no quarter" (no mercy) policy, and applied it not just to guerrillas (who soon retaliated in self-defense) but even to regular Confederate officers caught behind the lines. All that stood between the average Missourian and the firing squad was the local commander's whim. Halleck further ordered that Southern sympathizers in St. Louis be assessed for the relief of refugees streaming into the city from the war zones. Their plight was blamed 100% on Southern actions—and it was deemed only fair to make those guilty of only *words* or opinions pay for the *deeds* of others far away! Any who refused to pay were forcibly relieved of their goods, such as buggies, harness, pianos, and furniture. And the Union soon originated the practice, to be perfected by the Nazis and Soviets, of retribution against the kin of combatants. Halleck pronounced such Draconian measures "within the recognized laws of war"—seeming to have forgotten that the Union (as it itself was the first to insist) was not at war with Missouri. The unheard-of repressions were being "used by the U. S. government against citizens legally a part of the Union." Trade, travel, the press, life itself, limped along under revocable license of a corrupt, bigoted, irresponsible military bureaucracy.

The nation's press, during the Kansas troubles, had done itself proud showing the world that all Missourians were—in General/Senator Jim Lane's words—"wolves, snakes, devils." The Northern youth who'd taken in this gospel all but with his mother's milk was now a military misfit keeping his own opportune notion of "peace" in Missouri. The good troops went to the front lines; Missouri got the dregs—the "insubordinate and lawless."

Worst, of course, were the Kansans themselves. Missouri's horsethief enemies from of old were now power-brokers with the ear of the president, old brigands in patriotic new blue cynically "stealing themselves rich in the name of liberty." "These armed Kansas gangs swarmed through western and central Missouri cloaked with the authority of the Union army," creating "chaos and hatred that existed for years." Kansas towns waxed fat as communal receivers of stolen goods. Anything not nailed down was taken, from fence-rails to Bibles to *gravestones*.

The provisional government's "militia," meantime, far from defending the state, was wreaking its own havoc. This conscript force, the bottom of the ablebodied-manhood barrel, and usually stationed in its home neighborhood, "served as an excellent vehicle for local factions to settle old grudges." The least-offending citizen might find himself suddenly denounced and despoiled, even slain, for no other reason than the envy or spite of some lifelong ne'er-do-well, now a stalwart boy-in-blue. "In the area south of the Missouri River and along the Missouri-Kansas line, ruthless depredations by pro-Union troops reached tragic proportions."

Yet Newton's physical law applies also to human affairs: For every action there is an equal and opposite reaction. "A counterforce was gathering in the woods." Surrounded by such outrages, Confederates and neutrals alike began to hear the siren song of "a desire for an irregular military life" impossible to ignore. After Wilson's Creek, as we've seen, General Price let many of his Border soldiers go home to "look after their families"—and some, it was said, "did nothing else ever afterward." Like the Free French under Allied command in the 1940s, the Missourians fighting with Price in Mississippi grew mutinously frantic to go back and hit the hated foe on home ground. If the parallel sounds strained, it's because the Free French wound up on the winning side and so helped write the history books. Doubtless in either case it made better sense to go on obeying orders, submitting to a grand strategy; but the heartbreaks at home had a habit of issuing their own, higher orders.

And anyhow, as invaders have ever found out to their sorrow, guerrilla warfare *does* make military sense. Jomini, the Swiss military authority, defines guerrilla war as one in which the invader "holds scarcely any ground but that upon which he encamps." "Each armed inhabitant knows the smallest paths and their connections; he finds everywhere a relative or a friend who aids him; the commanders also know the country, and, learning immediately the slightest movements on the part of the invader, can adopt the best measures to defeat his projects." "By keeping in small bands," adds a Missourian, "they could move from place to place swiftly and secretly, or they could remain in a secluded camp a considerable period without attracting attention." "If they encountered a force they could not whip, they could run away from it." Even if they proved unable to protect their homes and loved ones, come the crunch, they'd have the solace of having been there and done their best. And, last but not least, they could wreak vengeance.

Mainline historians write of the Bushwhackers as if they sprang up in a vacuum—olympianly ignoring the mass injustice to which they were but the inevitable response. All was "roses," in their eyes —till the "bushes" reared their loathsome heads! Hatred of the enemy during the Civil War, they rightly point out, was confined "to the mountains of eastern Kentucky and Tennessee, and to the Missouri-Kansas border;" but they're wrong in adding, "the common denominator in these two widely separated areas was . . . widespread guerrilla activity." The latecomer Bushwhackers, they're saying, somehow set the seesaw of hatred going.

They have the cart before the horse. The "common denominator" was no more the guerrilla activity itself than it was the wilderness setting rendering it possible. It was the *unbearable political situation* unique to those areas. In Arkansas and Mississippi it was a tolerable if disreputable business making war on the Union; in

Kentucky and Missouri (states which in finespun Union theory had not seceded) it was a high crime. In the one you were a "belligerent," in the other an outlaw. Like all conquerors the Union would pacify rear areas with words, by making laws against resistance! And in a world where yesterday's robbers, rapists, arsonists, and murderers were the "law" and their victims criminals, criminality could be something to be proud of. Remember: There were Jayhawkers years before there were Bushwhackers. The Jayhawkers, and their Federal abettors, sowed the dragon's teeth; the Bushwhackers were the armed men who sprang up in the furrows.

In the modern popular mind, irregular warfare in the East was somehow nobler and more righteous. It's totally overlooked that the difference between glamorous John Mosby or John Hunt Morgan and villainous William Clarke Quantrill was one of degree not type. Swashbuckling Mosby, Virginia's exemplary "partisan ranger," who's had as many admirers as Jeb Stuart, in his day had as many bitter enemies as Quantrill; General Grant called for "any of Mosby's men" to be hanged without trial. Kentuckian Morgan and crew, captured in Ohio—in uniform—were tossed in the state penitentiary with the other "criminals." Time has cast a mellowing veil of romance over "guerrilla activity" east of the Mississippi. There were Bushwhackers in chivalrous Virginia. There just were no Jayhawkers.

"Of the many crosses President Lincoln had to bear during the war years, Missouri was assuredly one of the heaviest." Troubled by the inevitable excesses of his own military dictatorship, the president battled his generals for a just or at least consistent guerrilla policy. He caused a letter to be written, over the signature of Halleck, then U. S. Army general-in-chief, officially seeking the advice of Dr. Francis Lieber, of New York, a German-born savant "recognized for his study of the usages and customs of war."

Halleck must have privately gnashed his teeth. Himself a writer on military law, he was best-known to Missourians as the author of General Order No. 32, the "no quarter" order of December, 1861, which had "established the treatment for partisan Confederate soldiers"—a "treatment" potentially fatal to the "patients."

Lieber—himself a Radical, but reasonable—scandalized his Radical ilk. Publishing his conclusions as *Guerrilla Parties, Considered with Reference to the Laws and Usages of War,* he pointed out that the populace of the areas in question saw the Federal army as "the invader"—and resistance to invasion, far from outlawry, is rather a "rising of the people" ("the people in arms," as Clausewitz puts it; or "the legitimate bandit in conflict with conquest," as John N. Edwards more colorfully calls the Bushwhacker). The insurgents' sheer numbers, if nothing else, "entitled them to the full benefits of the law." The "invader" couldn't condemn them merely on the basis of their motive. Even uniforms weren't necessary, provided the civilian clothing worn was simply the guerrillas' everyday attire and not "for purposes of stealth or disguise."

The key, Lieber concluded, was whether they "operated in connection with the regular army and were enrolled as part of it," by virtue of their leaders' holding officers' commissions.

Like other West Pointers North and South, "Jefferson Davis did not believe in guerrilla warfare." Once U. S. secretary of war, himself a heroic, if frustrated, military officer, he liked to control all things personally—and guerrillas were by definition tricky to control. Nonetheless, on April 21, 1862, the Confederate Congress passed a Partisan Ranger Act, authorizing the president to commission officers to form partisan ranger bands. The Confederate War Department soon construed the act as passing the authority along to military department commanders; and three months later, on July 17, 1862, Trans-Mississippi Department commander General Thomas C. Hindman promulgated his own liberalized guerrilla order under the Richmond act, in effect legitimizing even spontaneously, previously formed Bushwhacker bands. In the same month he sent high-ranking recruiting officers north into occupied Missouri to harmonize and make the most of their operations.

"The result was a fierce flare-up of guerrilla operations all over the state." Small groups cut railways and attacked isolated Federal bands. Larger forces, up to 3,000, won a few fair-sized victories, most notably at Lone Jack near Kansas City on August 16.

Standard historians, who make much of Price's failure to raise 50,000 volunteers in 1861, have less to say of the Unionist provisional government's simultaneous call for 42,000, which yielded only 6,000. Now, responding to the guerrilla successes, in late July that government ordered the full mobilization of the Missouri State Militia, theoretically a state- but actually a Federal-controlled force.

The move played simplemindedly into Rebel hands. Total mobilization meant *every* ablebodied Missouri man 18 to 45 must

54

prepare to fight for the Union or be thrown in jail. Neutral or conservative Missourians, those of secret Southern sympathies, those with loved ones in the Confederate army, found themselves facing a desperate decision. The militia callup "sent many men fleeing to the brush"—into the arms of Hindman's recruiters or even the guerrilla life itself. Unoffensive average citizens swelled the hardcore ranks of committed Rebels and embittered Jayhawker victims: those with raw memories of "a father murdered . . . a brother waylaid and shot . . . a house pillaged"; who'd "seen the accumulation of a lifetime go up in smoke . . . their families thrust out upon the pitiless prairies . . . blooded stock [taken] to Kansas . . . a father's gray hairs dabbled in blood." "Hundreds of people," a Federal general wrote attorney general Edward Bates, "true and loyal men . . . have already been robbed . . . insulted and in many cases murdered by these troops from Kansas." Not only had "hundreds of good men" had to "fly to the bushes for protection," many were becoming Bushwhackers outright, "as a means of safety"! "They were not outlaws in the beginning," but were made outlaws by outrages without redress; "most of them went in with a wound that rankled." It insults the memory of these decent men, surely done enough wrong in their lifetimes, piously to hold that all would've been well had they only not had the effrontery to live—to put them all down as devils, as just so many Quantrills.

The "devil" himself, for that matter (and clearly Quantrill has served some people's need for devils), deserves reappraisal. His "devilishness" is less proven fact than simply a partisan opinion dinned into the popular mind by a century of repetition. The fullest account of his life was the hatchet-work of a Kansan, and only one well-known writer defended him at all in the postwar period. This was John N. Edwards, General Jo Shelby's good right arm, purple-prosed composer of his dispatches. Modern scholarly impatience with Edwards' flowery romanticism makes all too clear which side lost the war. Less clear is why moderns tend to embrace Edwards's romanticized picture of Shelby's "Iron Brigade" while scorning his corollary brief for Quantrill and Bushwhackers.

Northern shrillness against Quantrill perhaps originates in the fact that he was Northern himself, abolitionist even: one to whose awful treason diabolical motives must be assigned. One 1860 night some Jayhawkers came to Missouri slave-stealing. One of them—

Quantrill—puzzlingly warned the Missourians. Perhaps he was only winning a Missouri welcome, having worn his Kansas one thin; but thieves are queer ones to complain. Perhaps he was a mental case —certainly several of his men skirted psychopathy. But there are always madmen in our midst; and even madmen don't go bushwhacking without cause. Quantrill's own sanity, like anybody else's, may be judged by measuring his words against his deeds.

After fighting as a regular in the big battles of 1861, Quantrill had concluded that the South could never win that kind of war, already a war for sheer survival. "Everything connected with it was desperate," as Edwards points out; "the Southern people to succeed had to fight a desperate war." Only let the desperate, "no quarter" war be brought home to the North, Quantrill argued—and many, from immortal Stonewall Jackson to writer-editor J. D. B. DeBow, agreed —and the Northern public would repudiate the Lincoln government's policy of crushing the South. Indeed, this came far closer to happening in any case than most moderns dream.

Confederate officialdon recoiled from Quantrill's thesis, so bluntly put. Yet Quantrill himself must have impressed Jefferson Davis, for he carried away from Richmond in early 1862 a captain's commission for independent partisan service. And in that crucial midsummer, back in Missouri, his whole force was sworn into the Confederate army by Colonel Gideon W. Thompson. Later Price "probably issued Quantrill a field commission as colonel."

As the blazon of his policy, Quantrill "raised the black flag." Northern critics seem to have gleefully seized on this as outlawry or piracy, admitted and flaunted, a repudiation of the Stars and Bars. They were betraying their military ignorance. The black flag is simply the opposite of the *white* flag—the universal signal of "no quarter offered or sought." Quantrill was just being honest. It was the other side that was sailing under "false colors." On August 16, 1863, when he first broke out the black banner, the Federals had been offering "no quarter" for two years under red-white-and-blue! In General Blunt's baggage, captured at Fort Baxter, the Bushwhackers found the general's personal American flag sewn with a border of black silk, "which meant no quarter."

And being a signal, not an identity badge, the black flag was flown only as the occasion called for it. "If it were not unfurled, the fight took its chances." According to both Edwards and participant

John McCorkle, at infamous Centralia in 1864 *both* sides flew the black flag—literally—and behaved to match.

Other Bushwhacker earmarks included their "dress peculiar to themselves." Much like the plumage of other predators, it combined practicality with visual impact. "Its distinguishing item was a 'guerrilla shirt'," the ruffled, boldly embroidered contribution of some devoted Rebel sweetheart. In other respects the well-dressed guerrilla resembled the horsebacked Western plainsman.

The indispensable "accessory," of course, was "their superior weapon," the Colt revolving pistol, "the real secret of their success in combat against their more numerous enemy." Carrying from two to eight revolvers in their belts and on their saddles, and often extra cylinders in their pockets, the guerrillas actually invented the concept of overwhelming firepower, destined to reach full flower in World War I. Most Union troops on the Border in 1862 were still "armed only with single-shot muzzle-loading carbines, or muskets and sabers." Officers "complained continually of their weapons, and begged for revolvers for their men." Armchair critics scorned the guerrillas as "skulkers," shooters from ambush; in fact the typical Bushwhacker tactic was to charge, spectacularly as a knight in the lists, reins between teeth, a blazing sixgun in either hand.

Though the point is still stubbornly disputed, the guerrillas' combat value and effectiveness "has always been evident." Called "the greatest mounted military organization the world has ever known," they were a clear asset to their own side. When the regular Confederates forsook Missouri, early in 1862, they remained "the only representatives of the Southern cause in this quarter."

And they soon made themselves felt. That May the Quantrill band attacked entrenched Union garrisons from eastern Kansas to mid-Missouri. Harassment became unceasing and terrifying; "the most minor skirmishes were of a desperate nature." "Six mail carriers disappeared in one week between Independence and Kansas City. A load of hay to be safe had to have with it a company of cavalry. A messenger bearing an order required a company as an escort." In late summer the Bushwhackers saved the day for Confederate regulars at hard-fought Lone Jack. That fall they struck Shawneetown and Olathe in Johnson County, Kansas. Heading south for the winter, Quantrill joined regular Colonel Warner Lewis in an attack on Lamar's Union garrison. Repulsed with heavy losses from the fortlike courthouse, the angry Bushwhackers burned part of the town before continuing on South. Such, in briefest outline, was one short season's work for one guerrilla band—the most famous, granted, and yet but "one of dozens."

For the vast majority of Bushwhackers never became famous —or infamous. Clearly Jackson County's pride of place in Bush-whacker song and story owes less to Quantrill's own prominence than the reverse: Jackson County was populous and strategic; events there were crucial, involved large numbers, and were reported in detail. Logically the participants became nationally known.

Every Missouri county, however, had its Bushwhackers, those above all where Southern sympathy had always been strong—and where geography cooperated. Miles south of storied Jackson, down where the five slender wooded fingers of the Osage River's upper tributaries blocked the Border prairie, optimum conditions existed for "little war." Here smoldered struggles that were perhaps typical and all the bitterer in their very obscurity, because they were little and local, neighbor-against-neighbor. Here arose Bushwhackers perhaps truly representative in their sheer anonymity.

Anonymous, but not nobodies, by any means. The "average" guerrilla was no shiftless nonentity, but characteristically a prewar pillar of his community, a Confederate regular who slipped home to recruit, and found he "had to fight every jump in the road." It was an easy, inevitable step on into the Bushwhacker life.

Such a man was Captain William Henry Taylor. He'd resigned office as Vernon County sheriff to become quartermaster of the Seventh Cavalry, the county unit; he would be elected sheriff again after the war. His war experience was a mix of regular and irregular service. In midsummer, 1864, with only twelve men, he burned what Quantrill had left of Union-held Lamar; yet the fall found him alongside knightly Shelby on Price's great raid. Once he forced Archie Clements, Bloody Bill Anderson's dreaded "enforcer," to return stolen articles to an aged Vernon County citizen.

William Marchbanks, son of the judge who'd taken the depositions in the John Brown case, himself was a seasoned peace officer. In April, 1861, age 27, he was commissioned captain in the State Guard; a year later he "entered the Confederate service, and came up into Missouri to recruit." He soon found himself Vernon County's "best-loved" Bushwhacker. Yet his company fought as regulars during the 1864 raid. "The Federals who fought him," wrote a contemporary, "generally respect him." Once, he and his men let the Federal district commander, Colonel C. W. Blair, and his party finish their hunt and "return to Fort Scott unmolested" from their timber haunts. How many moderns—branding the Bushwhackers barbarians—would wage such chivalrous war?

Vernon County's premier soldier, Colonel Hunter himself, was a Bushwhacker according to some, including Edwards—a "still hunter," he calls him. Hunter slipped back into Missouri after the Pea Ridge defeat, mustering men and haunting lonely roads till "Federal detachments swore the devil was there." Still circuit and county clerk, carrying the courthouse keys on his campaigns, he hauled away the public records in a Confederate army wagon, saving them from burning with the town the next spring. These were Curtis's "reptiles," Lane's "snakes, wolves, devils"? It would bring laughter if it didn't come nearer bringing tears.

There's a grotesque irony in righteous latterday assertions of the unrelieved savagery of the Bushwhackers. While the guerrillas were at least *trying* to play by the rules of war (witness Quantrill's effort to exchange prisoners, spurned by the opposition), Federals were inventing "scorched earth" and the policy of reprisal against the innocent kin of combatants. It strains our own savage century's belief: Those infamous desperadoes of our schoolbooks fought for four long, bitter years without once making war on women! At Lawrence the Bushwhackers killed 150 men and boys without (despite great provocation) touching a single woman, though Northern propaganda would long shriek otherwise. At Fort Baxter they behaved as if the lone enemy woman present was simply invisible. Friendly or neutral "ladies" they treated with sweeping courtesy. Amazingly, Southerners emerged from the lost war with their chivalry intact. Northerners—as only befitted believers in "equality"—had long outgrown such "discrimination."

At the same time, Southern women played a far more direct part in the struggle than their supposedly "freer" Northern sisters. Chivalry by no means meant restricting valor to men. Far from it— "Knights of the Bush"logically inspired their "lady Bushwhackers." Not pretending to be men, not shooting it out with bluecoats, they served as women have always served (in peace *and* war), as auxiliaries—"scouts, spies, guides and couriers."

Southeast Vernon County in particular produced its Confederate heroines. Ella Mayfield, her Bushwhacker brothers Brice and "Crack" slain early in the war, saved their comrade John McNeil—a man she'd never seen before—by tearfully telling the Springfield provost marshal he was her lover. Her young sisters Sallie and Jennie, arrested in 1864, daringly escaped from the women's prison in downtown St. Louis. The Mayfield girls and Eliza Gabbert buried the seven Bushwhackers slain at the Gabbert house in May, 1863. "Ella Mayfield with her own hands" gathered and assembled the pieces of Bill Bridgman's shattered skull "and smoothed the hair over the wounds to hide their ghastliness." Dropping her shovel she then rode 125 miles in twenty-four hours searching out and delivering evidence to save another man's life. Once, armed with her husband's revolver, she hid from Federal militiamen in a lonely thicket for two days without food or water. "The women and girls of that neighborhood at that day did not faint at the smell or gunpowder or human blood, or shrink from the sight of a dead man," wrote a late-Victorian, when ladies *did* faint and shrink. "The work performed by the Southern women during the war will never be understood fully," summed up Edwards. And they performed it, be it remembered, in long skirts and petticoats.

Of both sexes and all ages, the Bushwhackers "were of great service to the Confederate cause." "While they brought ruin upon many a Southern family by their presence, they kept many a Federal soldier from being sent to the front to shoot against the Southern armies in Arkansas and Mississippi." Besides diverting troops from the front, they "continually sent valuable information to Southern generals . . . frequently served with regular Confederate forces . . . and rendered invaluable service as scouts and guides."

Never were there more than 3,000 or 4,000 Bushwhackers scattered over Missouri; yet an estimated 27,000 persons, on both sides, were to lose their lives in the state through their stubborn struggle. And as early as midsummer, 1862, they were tying down some *60,000* Union troops—four times the total with which Grant was invading Tennessee at about the same time!

"BACK HOME, APRIL, 1865" - *Tom Lea*

# SIX
## *The Burnt District*

Worsening western Missouri's wartime plight was the presence, just to its east, of the Missouri hill counties, of divided sentiments, often even pro-Union, and always contrary. "Far removed and practically beyond the range of vision of the civilized world," for example, Cedar County had first raised the "Stockton Grays" for Confederate service—but soon earned a reputation as "that Valley of the Shadow of Death for isolated or belated Confederate travelers," and seen its seat torched by none other than Jo Shelby.

Adjoining southeastern Vernon County, then, found itself *another* sort of border: the Kansas Border's backside, so to speak. Timbered Montevallo and Dover townships have always had a reputation for breeding hard, rough men. Perhaps it stemmed from their sense of their beset, surrounded Southernness, for no other neighborhood so seethed with fiery Southern sentiment.

In the winter of 1861-62, Captain Henry Taylor took leave of Price's army, came back and set about raising a second company around Montevallo, where James M. Gatewood had already raised a first. As ever in such conditions, without pause, recruiting became fighting. In March, when eager Confederate units joined in a costly

61

attack on Unionist Humansville, Taylor's force "covered the retreat and saved the command." In early April Dade countian Colonel John T. Coffee, one of the key Trans-Mississippi recruiters, made a "stirring speech" in the Montevallo Academy, garnering 70 recruits (in a town of perhaps 200) for Taylor's company.

The company was still at Montevallo on April 14 when two companies of the First Iowa Cavalry, stationed at ravaged Osceola, took notice. Taylor himself was surprised and captured "while eating breakfast at a house four miles southwest." The captainless Confederates in the town itself managed to slip away in the dusk, and the Iowans took over, headquartering in Scobey's Hotel.

At 4:30 A.M. they awoke to find themselves surrounded and under attack by a motley force mostly of civilians, actually led by local hotelkeeper Wilson Maddox. Sporadic shooting went on till dawn, when the ghostly besiegers melted away.

Fearing further attacks, Iowan Colonel Moss ordered his men to pull out—and leave the town in ashes behind them. The hotels, the stores, even the Academy (Vernon County's first and still only secondary school, state-chartered in 1855)—collapsed in flames in a few barbaric minutes. After all, Moss said, they'd been "used as places of protection and resort by the guerrillas."

It was a lethal blow to the settlement. The new Montevallo that grew up after the war, a bit over a mile east, was new indeed. *Old* Montevallo went back to brush or under the plow.

And it was a senseless, shortsighted act of arson. A frontier culture could not be fatally weakened by the mere burning of its towns, its real heart being the surrounding farflung farms and the "bush" itself—the Bushwhackers' true "places of protection and resort." The Federals weren't heeding Clausewitz: Guerrilla warfare, he wrote, required "a scattered distribution of houses and farms, rather than a population concentrated in villages." Colonel Coffee was still recruiting around charred Montevallo in August. By then he'd gathered some 400 men, each aflame with the burning new motive of revenge. Repeatedly "Coffee for breakfast" headed the Federals' menu, and repeatedly "Coffee was served" "hot and strong" "before they were ready for him." Unionists dared not set foot in the neighborhood save in bristling force.

As 1863 dawned, the deadlock approached the unbearable. "The record of that year is one of murders, arsons, robberies, and outrages." "There were no holidays and no Sundays; no courts, no schools, no religious meetings." "Back and forth into Missouri rode the Kansas jayhawkers; back and forth into Kansas rode the Missouri guerrillas; back and forth into loyal Cedar rode the Vernon bushwhackers; back and forth into rebel Vernon rode the Cedar militia." The few families struggling to lead normal lives "had a hard time of it. They were preyed upon by both sides."

In March, seeking to shore up their shaky communications between Fort Scott and such Missouri garrison towns as Springfield, through the rebellious "Border tier", the Federals sponsored the setting up of a small militia unit in Vernon County. Augustus Baker, a "conservative Union man," was elected captain.

His rival, John Frizzell, "took his defeat in great ill humor." A few evenings after the election, he and a friend called at Baker's house—almost right on the Border—"putting on a smooth exterior and assuming extreme friendliness." Once inside Frizzell jerked out his revolver and fired pointblank at Baker, who fell back dying in his wife's arms. Troopers from Fort Scott arrested Frizzell at a friend's home in Cedar County. Martial law overriding constitutional quibbles about venue, he was taken back to Fort Scott and tried by court-martial, convicted, and sentenced to hang in late May.

To give testimony for a stay of execution, hoping to prove Frizzell was somewhere else on the evening of the murder, Major A. J. Pugh led a party of some half-dozen militiamen from Cedar County to Fort Scott, by the main road through Nevada.

In the timber along Big Drywood Creek, a scout pricked up his ears and galloped off to alert Captain William Marchbanks to the passage and probable return of the small enemy force. The Bushwhacker, with "nineteen of his best men," was camped on the creek south of the Marmaton. He'd been joined by the band of another, shadier breed of guerrilla leader named James N. "Pony" Hill—"a desperate character, a hard case since boyhood." Failing to cut off Pugh's homing party at the Drywood ford, Marchbanks and Hill determined to follow on and bushwhack it at Nevada.

Riding stealthily up through the Little Drywood timber, the Bushwhackers burst in at the southwest corner of the square, firing and Rebel-yelling. The Federals had stopped to rest at a brick hotel on the south side of the square. Several scurried on inside; the rest scattered to the north. Leaving part of his band besieging the hotel,

Marchbanks gave chase with the remainder. "Near where the old jail stood," he wrote, "we overhauled them. One took shelter in a house" two blocks east—an old man named Shuey, "dismounted, unarmed, and terror-stricken," it was said. "'Pony' Hill and Oliver Burch killed him." Marchbanks himself dropped a second, named Whitley, in a dead-end lane in an exchange of gunfire, according to his own report; others had him shooting him out of his saddle at the northeast edge of town. Amazingly the other militiamen escaped unscathed. The Bushwhackers lost only a horse.

A trifling ripple amid the clash of giant armies, it was a crisis in the lives of those involved. When Pugh and his men reached their homes and reported the attack, "a fierce cry for vengeance and retaliation went up among the militia of Cedar and St. Clair." Soon some 100 "well armed and mounted" militiamen had fallen in under the command of Captain Anderson Morton of Taberville, "a prudent and skilful leader" who "knew the country" and the enemy "thoroughly." (Modern Taberville sources call him "not well thought of," "little better than a horsethief." Reportedly he slew a personal enemy, branded "disloyal"—and then married the widow!)

According to tips received, the guerrilla camp was on Moore's Branch, south of Nevada. Clearly the townsfolk kept them furnished with provisions and information. Clearly, when the hapless militiamen rode in, "a mesenger had at once sped away to the bushwhackers' camp with the tidings." (No evidence supports this; the Bushwhackers were all non-Nevadans.) The avengers, then, would first wipe out the camp, "and then march on the 'Bushwhacker capital,' as they called Nevada City, and give it to the torch."

Morton and his force left Taberville the evening of May 25, a bare thirty hours after the bushwhacking. Dawn found them on Moore's Branch, some three miles south of Nevada, beating the bushes but finding "no bushwhackers or signs of any." Irritably Morton called in his men. "The game had flown." But the town "yet remained to be disposed of." The place was to be "baptized with fire." Bushwhackers were to be "slain without mercy," but all "peaceable citizens" scrupulously spared (though how to tell the one from the other was not made clear), "no women insulted." "All buildings big enough for a bushwhacker to sleep in"—surely a broad enough definition—"were to be burned," "but no spoil was to be taken, all household goods were to be spared."

64

"Nevada City," if hardly a city, was a thriving hamlet of perhaps 450 souls—on paper, anyhow. Reality was anyone's guess. Some houses sheltered fugitives, squatters; "the owners with their families had gone into the Southern Confederacy." Still the community's Southern tone held sway, undaunted and defiant. On the one hand "society was somewhat refined and exclusive"; on the other dram-shops were patronized "to their fullest capacity." There were no churches—typically of a Southern county seat, taverns preceded temples. The senior business enterprise was Wilson's Saloon, where the house whiskey "actually froze up during a moderate winter"! Geezers over their well-watered drams and matrons over their back fences alike boasted of their brave boys in gray far away at the front. The few "loyalists"—real or "claimed-to-be"—rated as mere harmless cranks. Rebel or loyal, "not more than a dozen adult male residents" remained. The "Bushwhacker capital," on Tuesday, May 26, 1863, was more nearly a "housewives' capital."

The women were waking as the hundred bluecoats rode in from the timber, up along Adams Street, then the main road from the south. They scattered; some, including Morton, requisitioned break-fast from would-be Union sympathizers; others stole the makings, such as "real coffee." Predictably, a search for Bushwhackers turned up nothing. At nine o'clock muster was held on the square; the burning orders were repeated. The troopers then fanned out over the town in squads of three or four, quietly, "without yelling and whooping, no dashing about, no boisterous conduct of scarcely any sort," knocking on doors like solicitors or missionaries:

"We are going to burn this house. Get your things out in twenty minutes. If you want any help, we will help you, but the house must be burned. This damned Rebel den shall be destroyed!"

"No pleadings availed. The tears of sorrowful females were as useless as the maledictions of the enraged ones." Torches were set to the buildings as quickly as the occupants could be turned out into the streets. "Soon bright flames flashed from the burning buildings all over the town. The dooryards and vacant lots were piled with household articles," around which the evicted women "wailed and mourned, or scolded and stormed," while they "kept the flying brands from their goods, or quarreled with the torch bearers."

Courthouse, stores, all other public buildings were total losses save the schoolhouse and the jail, both damaged. "In all about 75 houses, with their outbuildings, were burned." A few small homes of Union sympathizers were spared. Captain Henry Taylor, happening to be in town as a paroled prisoner, saw his house go up in flames, though he himself was "saved by the compass and square" when Morton found he was a fellow Mason. No lives were lost, and there were only trifling reports of violence. However provoked, however surrounded by and inured to the horrors of war, the militiamen seem to have managed marked restraint.

At eleven o'clock, as the militia rode out, down the Montevallo road, "volumes of black, thick smoke" rolled up into the blue May sky behind them. Women and children sat crying in the streets amid their strewn worldly all. Flames were dying down over the ruins. "Alas for Nevada City! The bright little town of the prairies had become an expanse of glowing coals. In one short hour she had been smitten by the hot and heavy hand of war. Thenceforward for two long years she was to sit solitary amidst her ashes; thorns and brambles were to come up in her gardens and streets. The few houses, untenanted and shunned, would but add to her loneliness." The dazed folk would seek shelter with kin in the country, or in faraway Federal garrison towns . . . or holes in the ground.

On their way home Morton's men ran afoul a band of Vernon County Bushwhackers, themselves homecoming from a raid on Cedar County, where they'd burnt some of the militiamen's own homes. It was that kind of grimly-neighborly war.

Just ten days later, the Federals conceded the failure of their ferocious "pacification" policies in the time-honored way—by redoubling them! Two occupation jurisdictions were set up: the District of the Border, comprising the two westernmost tiers of Missouri Border counties north of the 38th parallel, plus adjacent Kansas, headquartered in Kansas City and commanded by General Thomas C. Ewing, predictably an ambitious Kansas political hack; and the District of the Frontier, making up the same longitudinal range south of 38 (the Congressional township baseline crossing northern Vernon County), commanded by Colonel Charles W. Blair and headquartered at Fort Scott. At midsummer Blair sent four companies of the Third Wisconsin Cavalry to man "picket posts" at key Vernon County river crossings. Prudently avoiding the fierier Rebel areas, they saw little action, and soon were finding the Rebel girls more rewarding objects of pursuit than the Rebel boys.

66

"Pacification" was also failing farther south. In Jasper County, stamping-ground of Bushwhacker Ed Shirley—another judge's son —the county seat went the way of its ancient namesake: *Cartago delenda est,* Federals and Rebels seemed to agree. While both the town and Shirley himself were casualties, the "pacifiers" gained nothing. Carthage had to be treated to a second burning a few months hence, and Shirley's place was taken by his sister Myra Maybelle, an unusually unforgiving "lady Bushwhacker" destined to go down in history as Belle Starr, the Bandit Queen.

On August 14, an old brick building in Kansas City, on Grand Avenue between 14th and 15th streets, where the "army of freedom" imprisoned women under arrest without warrant or charges for the "crime" of having male Bushwhacker relatives, collapsed. Four young women were crushed to death, one fatally injured, others seriously hurt. Among the dead were Cole Younger's cousin Charity Kerr, and Josephine, sister of William "Bloody Bill" Anderson; Mary, a second sister, only 16, was "so disfigured that when those dearest to her dug her out of the wreck they did not know her." Malicious neglect, if not mischief, was widely rumored.

So far an unremarked Quantrillite, Anderson became "bloody" indeed. The fragmented bands came together in a vengeful bolt of Bushwhacker fury. Lawrence, the enemy's heart, home of hated Jim Lane, was the target. On August 21, 1863, Quantrill's 300-plus Bushwhackers, joined by 100-odd Confederate regulars under Colonel John D. Holt, slew some 150 Lawrence men and boys and destroyed $1,500,000 in property, but harmed not a woman. The raiders not only remembered their own dead womenfolk but made "Remember Osceola!" their battle cry. They searched hard but fruitlessly for Hugh Fisher, pious looter of Osceola altar furnishings; as well as for Jim Lane, who saved himself by scampering half-naked into a cornfield; other men survived by crouching, rather ungallantly, under their women's skirts. "Not one Kansan sold his life dearly." "The ladies of Lawrence were brave and plucky," said Quantrill, "but the men . . . were a pack of cowards." (The women, of course, had less to fear.) The Bushwhackers lost a lone man, who was left behind, near dead-drunk on his horse.

Already General Order Number Ten (August 18) had given notice of Federal plans for the Border. The depopulation scheme —surely the first instance, the *invention,* of "ethnic cleansing," as it's now called—was hatched well before the Lawrence raid; Lawrence only touched it off. It was due to political arm-twisting from the discountenanced Lane that General Ewing on August 26 at last issued the malevolent General Order Number Eleven.

The decree "completed the ruin of western Missouri." All countrydwellers in the District of the Border's western half (Jackson, Cass, Bates, and northern Vernon counties) must quit their homes within fifteen days, "regardless of their innocence or guilt in aiding the guerrillas." All houses and outbuildings must be burned and all grain stores removed to Federal garrison towns or destroyed. Piling insult on injury, the Fifteenth Kansas Cavalry—the "Redlegs," Blunt's "Forty Thieves," commanded by Jennison, late of the jayhawking Seventh—was called in to carry out the edict. The debauched, vicious Kansans had a field day, as melodramatically depicted in George Caleb Bingham's famed painting. "Men were shot down in the very act of obeying the order," wrote Bingham, who was there. "Dense columns of smoke arising in every direction marked the conflagrations of dwellings. Giant wagon-trains, miles in length," heavy with the worldly goods of the newly homeless, rolled Kansas-wards. The Border had a new name: the Burnt District. Long honored as the "sire" of the finest stolen Missouri horses, Jennison gained new ill-fame. For years to come Missourians knew the forlorn chimneys of burned houses as "Jennison Monuments."

The Order—as usual—fell hardest on the innocent. Those it supposedly targeted, on the other hand, felt it hardly at all. "The immediate effectiveness of Order No. 11 was practically nil." Popular support was "not that important to Quantrill," who rode as rampant as ever in scorched rural Jackson County. On October 6 he bushwhacked a Federal wagon-train near Fort Baxter in southeast Kansas, killing 80 for a loss of three, and all but capturing General Blunt. In places, moreover, such as northern Vernon County, the Border was growing harder to hurt; "there was nothing left to burn." Pickings grew so poor the Jayhawkers turned their larcenous eyes toward future Oklahoma and its beleaguered Indians.

Early in 1864 a scandal broke at Fort Scott, involving "disloyal fort personnel" and "numerous attractive young women from Vernon and Barton counties in Missouri," spying and smuggling ammunition. The episode, boasted a Kansas writer, "reflected the desperate efforts of the Confederates to recover" from the conse-

68

**"ORDER NO. 11"** - *George Caleb Bingham*

quences of the Order "that had cleared the western Missouri Border counties of guerrilla sanctuary." The story sounds suspiciously like whistling past the graveyard. "The rebels [still] control the country-side," conceded the Unionist *Kansas City Journal* on August 13. *1864* The Border, and the Bushwhackers, were battling on.

On September 16, 1864, Price reentered Missouri with a large army, bent on capturing St. Louis or some other key place. If he'd come in blazing, Bushwhacker style, he might well have succeeded, but his plodding, regular-army progress soon reduced the "invasion" to a mere foraging and recruiting raid. As Price swung west, the guerrillas joined him as scouts and auxiliaries. The newly-demonic Anderson had eclipsed Quantrill in charismatic leadership. Northerners would remember "Centralia" (September 27) as the heinous massacre of twenty-six wounded Union prisoners, forgetting that it was also a standup fight between two black-flag-flying forces, likened by participant Frank James to Thermopylae. Nearly every one of the 160 Union troops engaged was killed. It was the one Southern success of the campaign, save that at the Big Blue crossing in Jackson County on October 22, where Colonel Hunter and his

Borderers, then with Jackman, did some of the hardest fighting. Next day at Westport, the tide turned forever. The Confederates streamed south, hounded by huge converging blue hordes, and were further smashed at Mine Creek in Linn County, Kansas, in one of the largest cavalry actions of the war, on October 25—tenth anniversary and reenactment of berserker Balaclava.

It was the only regular Confederate foray into Kansas, and the Missourians "were taking advantage of the fact to extract revenge for jayhawker depredations against their friends and relatives." At the same time, "infuriated Kansans . . . murdered and maltreated Confederate prisoners." "The old game of atrocities followed by reprisals was on again." Trading Post town—shades of '58 and the Marais des Cygnes Massacre—suffered anew.

The end of the long, disastrous day saw the shattered Rebel ranks crossing back into Missouri in southern Henry and northern Richland townships in northwest Vernon County, making for Douglass Ford over the Marmaton, where alone the train of some 500 wagons could cross. Shelby's Iron Brigade, seconded by Hunter's local men, many actually unarmed, fought a desperate, successful rearguard action at Charlot Prairie near the Border, where cannon fire turned the dusky prairie to "an ocean of flames."

"The bulk of the army, 10,000 men or more, got across the Marmaton and rested a few hours at Deerfield" near the 1861 skirmish site. Price himself catnapped in the house of pioneer settler William Modrel just west of town. After the nightlong nightmarish traffic jam at the ford, the encumbering wagon train—long a "millstone around the army's neck"—was at last ordered destroyed; precious supplies went up in flames or were overturned in the river; the prairie was strewn with discarded revolvers and muskets and freed horses and mules; cannons, at least according to local legend, were thrust into deep waters or old wells.

The Federals, meantime, were in Fort Scott, helping it celebrate. The place had been close to panic before Mine Creek's decision—"a speculative person with $100 cash could have bought and paid for the entire town"—and relief was proportionately great. Next day, minuetlike, the Rebels resumed their flight, south past Lamar and Carthage, and the Federals their pursuit. The rearguard Iron Brigade won a final victory at Newtonia on October 28, but it was too late to matter. The Rebel remnant at last made it back to

Texas, some, with Shelby, never to surrender but to sink their flag and march on to Mexico; others lost heart and plodded homeward, each slowly reduced to thinking only of himself.

The Bushwhackers had stuck with Price till after Mine Creek. Now many straggled on to Texas either with the regulars or on their own. Bill Anderson had wound up as bloody in death as in life on October 26. In January Quantrill left the state for Kentucky and his own gruesome death. And in that cruelest April the home-wending rank-and-file hid and waited. The end was near, surely.

The end was near—for the righteous, for the fortunate. Peace of a sort was at hand for Missouri, for all the poor, ravaged Southland and her tattered, surrendering heroes—but not for Bushwhackers, those "reptiles," those "wolves, snakes, devils."

Union generals worried that the Rebel army would fragment into guerrilla bands and carry on indefinite partisan warfare—and "the Confederates' refusal to consider the guerrilla alternative may be a major reason why the South lost the Civil War" ("I am too old to go bushwhacking," was Lee's explanation). Clearly their refusal was fueled not simply by their chivalry or humaneness but also by their fear of the effect of further social breakdown on Southern race relations. Indeed, they wouldn't hesitate to resort to it in Reconstruction days, in defense of white supremacy.

On April 15, six days after Lee's surrender, a baby-faced Bushwhacker led six comrades into Lexington, Missouri, under a white flag, bent on following their general-in-chief's faraway example. Eight sullen, drunken Kansas and Wisconsin troopers opened fire. The boy leader took a bullet through the lung.

Diehard debunkers deny it ever happened, though the honester historical judgment is that it did. And if it didn't, it should have; for such things, and worse, were happening at every hand. Only, not all the casualties were named Jesse James.

## SEVEN
### *The Dead Men*

The Jayhawkers were going home to their hearthsides, honored veterans of the good fight, already embroidering their patriotic deeds for the future boredom of their grandchildren. But for their Missouri counterparts, as Jesse James had found, there was no going home.

James had been trying to surrender. He wouldn't try again. In southern Missouri, in the postwar decades, nightriding bands such as the Ku Klux Klan ofttimes were known as "the Dead Men," no doubt because they passed themselves off to superstitious ex-slaves as the ghosts (accounting for the white sheets) of the Confederate fallen. "They were dead men, most of them, moving among the living as ghosts," wrote Walter Hines Page; "and yet, as ghosts in a play, they held the stage." For many, the name had a painful aptness. They were the *other* Confederate dead: soldiers denied their soldierhood, damned as outlaws. What had they to lose, then? Outlaws they were called? Outlaws they'd be!

The near-fatal wounding of the soon-to-be Outlaw King under a white flag was no idle, insignificant event. It exemplified the plight of hundreds of Missourians—indeed, of the state itself. Even as the bullet struck, a new Constitutional Convention, packed (thanks to the "loyalty oath" disfranchising half the electorate) with Radicals, was meeting in St. Louis. Its "controlling spirit" was shifty Charles D. Drake, ex-Whig, ex-Know-Nothing, ex-Democrat, now the "typical Radical," who "hated all rebels, and hated conservatives more than rebels," and who "absolutely dominated his timid and inferior colleagues." The Convention—not the war—would prove "the high-water mark of hatred and fear in Missouri affairs."

The "Radicals" were the extremist Republicans seekng to prolong the wartime social disorder for their own benefit, political and economic. "Reconstruction" had a headstart in Missouri. Here the Radicals learned the lessons they would apply to all the South.

Clear back in 1861 General Fremont had put the army to work, not fighting Rebels, but wresting slaves from their lawful Missouri owners. Instantly overridden by the president, Fremont's order continued to be flaunted and enforced by Jayhawkers.

The issue remained acute, for Missouri's slaves were exempt from Lincoln's own wartime Emancipation Proclamation. Thus the Convention's first step, taken in January, 1865, was to leap to the head of the abolitionist parade, making Missouri the first slave state to abolish slavery on its own initiative. Abolition-with-compensation had been a popular topic in the Border states while the war went poorly for the North. Granted slaveowners had never shown much enthusiasm; yet any who might have remained "loyal" in honest expectation of compensation now found themselves ruined—as ruined as the rabidest Rebel. The Radicals were magically turning the conservatives' capital into Radical voters!

Then, "fearful that its good works might be undone by unsympathetic incumbents," the Convention voted the so-called "ousting ordinance," vacating as of May 1, 1865, the positions of all judges, county clerks, circuit attorneys, sheriffs, and recorders—completing the ideological purge of society's "natural leaders" begun in the war. Unfinished terms would be filled by appointees of the governor, a Drake stooge. The ordinance "dislodged some 800 officials." When the Missouri Supreme Court ruled it unconstitutional, the Radicals simply "had members of that bench forcibly removed"—arrested and bodily hauled out of their offices by militiamen!

Next, the Convention devised the "Ironclad Oath"—"much harsher than the wartime test oath"—intended to keep "disloyal" men out of not only public office and political function but also the licensed professions, corporate offices, the schoolroom, even the pulpit. Eighty-six kinds of deeds—including "feeling sympathy" for Rebels—were termed "disloyal." Included, of course, was anyone "who has ever been engaged in . . . that description of marauding commonly known as bush-whacking." To add brass to iron, "No one could vote who could not take the oath prescribed by the instrument upon the adoption of which the vote was taken." "The best men in the state were disfranchised." (Certainly Democrats were!) "A more inhuman, atrocious, and barbarous instrument . . . was never invented." In 1867 the U. S. Supreme Court would find it to be both a bill of attainder and an ex-post-facto law, both prohibited by the Federal Constitution, Article I, Section 10.

The state on which these repressions were being heaped was not in revolt. No public danger lurked, too awful to be coped with by constables. The people were too exhausted and impoverished for "disloyalty" 86 profligate ways. Along the Border, county governments had fairly ceased to exist. In Cass County not "600 inhabitants remained" out of the 10,000 of 1860. Jasper County had an eighth of its 1860 population. "Vernon County was a desert"; hardly "a hundred families" remained. Bates County had "not a single family left." There were no stores, no schools, no churches, no courts, almost no houses. And to this appalling desolation civilian refugees and Confederate soldiers wearily brought home their own needs and despair, many trudging hundreds of miles.

The impoverished, devastated state at once found itself being further crushed by the Radicals' aggressive economic program, designed to change the whole purpose of law and government. Conservative Missouri had always believed in limited, frugal government; but the new, "progressive" elements wanted government not simply to keep the peace, as traditionally, but actively to spur commercial growth at taxpayer expense. They virtually gave the state's huge equity in existing railroads to private interests—"meekly surrendered the public's lien against the prewar companies, saddling the people (rather than the rail companies) with the old $25 million debt." Formerly voters had had the right to approve bond issues for railroads and other improvements; but the new constitution put that right in the hands of local officials, such as county court judges, who could be arm-twisted or bribed.

The result was a statewide binge of bonded indebtedness. By

1870 Vernon County's railroad bond debt was a frightening 10.5 percent of its total property value, with the interest mounting alarmingly. Taxpayers began to rebel. In Nevada "a mass meeting threatened the judges that payment of any interest on the bonds 'would be at their peril.'" In self-defense the judges resigned—but Radical state officials refused to recognize their resignations. In St. Clair County, where angry mobs had seized and burned the public records, the court met for months in secret places, dodging federal marshals. Not till the next century would the issue be settled, when the U. S. Supreme Court ruled that Missouri counties must pay off the hated old bonds to the unoffending investors who by then held them. The last such bond wasn't retired till 1940.

Nowhere did the "culture war" rage more fiercely than in the schools. The Radicals' modern champions hold up their imposition of public schools as their proudest, happiest achievement, ignoring the furious opposition it encountered. Early Missouri subscribed to "what some called the 'Southern attitude' toward education," reflecting "the belief that public schools existed for the children of the poor; their maintenance was a type of state philanthropy, a necessary expense to be held to a minimum. Those who could afford it sent their children to private academies."

The "Southern attitude" was hostility not to education, as critics claimed, but to a certain *kind* of education. (Indeed, the pre-Civil War South had more colleges and academies, proportionately, than the North, and cultured Northerners found their Southern counterparts more broadly educated.) "Parents assumed major responsibility for the education of their children in the old order. The most common pattern of formal schooling before the Civil War was the subscription school, in which groups of parents retained a teacher." Union victory "created a unique opportunity at the state level for the champions of change to impose an educational revolution."

"Civil society exists for the creation of material resources," a public-school advocate baldly stated. (Tradition, by contrast, held that civil society exists for the moral improvement of man and to instill wisdom leading to a fuller understanding and appreciation of the Creator; as the Baltimore Catechism puts it, the purpose of life is "to know and love God.") The new schools would *"stamp out traditional work patterns, impose the industrialists' work values, and get children to internalize the new values as their own."* Schools

75

would be simply another kind of "factories," designed to *increase an individual's wants, encourage people to buy things, and thus stimulate markets"* (emphasis added). Schools must be "secular" and "utilitarian," preached "the father of public education," Horace Mann. All this was a far cry from the "Southern attitude" that schools should teach, not mere utility, but "character and grace." The charter of the Montevallo Academy (1855), for instance, proclaimed as its "only object" "the promotion of sound morals, pure literature and classical education"; it should be "under the influence of the Christian church," though strictly nonsectarian.

Perceptive moderns acknowledge the new schools' achieved aims—and deplore them: "The techniques taught . . . are not for [the child's] personal benefit but to make him an apt worker in a system resting on values that go counter to the attainment of personal welfare. True, the techniques enable the child to make a living in adulthood, but . . . only in a scheme laid down and enforced by a money economy and machine technology. Little of what is taught in schools is taught to enable the child to *live."*

Where formerly only parents had paid school taxes, the Radicals imposed the tax on all property owners—and school boards were empowered to levy them without voter approval!

Bitterly traditionalists fought back. The new public schools were widely boycotted, even after the Radicals made attendance compulsory. Private and religious alternatives sprang into being, including many of the state's now venerable colleges and preparatory schools. The "culture war" entered all phases of life and went on for decades—indeed, it goes right on today.

Such was the broader struggle behind the "outlaw phenomenon" for which Missouri—the "Robber State"—was best-known in the postwar years. The Radicals' social tinkerings exacerbated and prolonged the breakdown of law and order left by the war, creating a climate in which ordinary lawbreakers throve—and vigilante action inevitably followed. Usually composed of the "best men," the "natural leaders," vigilante bands in most cases acted with remarkable restraint—and discrimination. While ridding the community of real, undoubted criminals, they somehow overlooked another kind of outlaws: what would come to be called "political" offenders. Themselves ground down by Yankee banks and railroads, robbed by Radical tax collectors, their children seduced by Radical propaganda in the schools, ordinary, law-abiding men looked on *this* class of outlaws with understanding and even sympathy. Weren't they simply old comrades from the war, carrying on the fight against the old enemy in his new, more insidious form?

"No men ever strove harder to put the past behind them" than the Bushwhackers, insisted John N. Edwards, though the point is fanatically disputed. "They were not permitted to do so." Hidden and nursed by Southern sympathizers, Jesse James recovered from his lung wound to become the chief of a hard core of old Quantrill hands and their younger kinsmen, including brother Frank and the four Youngers, whose upstanding father had been robbed in 1861 and waylaid in 1862 by bluecoats. On February 14, 1866, the James gang "invented" bankrobbery, striking the Clay County Savings and Loan of Liberty, first in a long streak of successes. Another gang had already "invented" train robbery, back in Indiana, but the Missourians soon took the lead in that field as well.

The Missouri outlaw throve because he was no ordinary outlaw. Like every successful "outlaw"—like the Bushwhackers during the war—he was flesh-and-blood of the folk around him. He was the final upswelling of Lieber's "rising of the people"; Clausewitz's "people in arms"; Edwards' "legitimate bandit in conflict with conquest." His forays took him into other states, but seldom far outside his homeland. It says much that the James-Younger gang's undoing was its overreaching raid on Northfield, Minnesota.

The "Robin Hood" rationale of Jesse James and his ilk holds at least a grain of truth. Most ex-Rebels managed, despite all, to remain lawabiding men; but "Reconstruction" weighed on them for just what it was—a foreign occupation. And the outlaws were their late comrades-in-arms. The living Dead Men, as it were, of the old, lost cause, they could no more be betrayed than could the buried dead. It was for more than one reason that the nightriders wore sheets. The uniform of *this* army was a shroud.

The Jameses and Youngers were sons of Clay and Jackson counties respectively; but the war had made them at home all along the Border. The Youngers had kin in the timbered Ozark foothills around Osceola, and they themselves found this backwoods neighborhood inviting. Local folk wouldn't soon forget Lane's rape of Osceola in 1861—or that Jameses and Youngers had ridden with their avengers at Lane's Lawrence two years later.

"A growing army of detectives ran up against a stone wall of silence. By now the bankers of several states had called in the Pinkerton National Detective Agency to aid in the hunt, but the men sent from Pinkerton headquarters in Chicago were poorly received in rural Missouri." "The Pinkertons had been used by the Union armies to spy on Confederates and by the big corporations to spy on workers; now they were being used by the banks to spy on the James brothers. It was not a reputation likely to quell the country people's ingrained suspicions of city slickers."

The Pinkertons received a tip about the Youngers' St. Clair County hideout, and two undercover Pinkerton operatives ("paid assassins," says Edwards) set out. Posing as "horse and cattle buyers"—a masquerade that fooled no one—the Pinkertons on March 17, 1874, reached Roscoe, a small town on the way to Monegaw Springs, the bandits' hideout; they were accompanied by a local deputy sheriff, an ex-Union soldier. That afternoon the three lawmen rode up to the farmhouse of Theodrick Snuffer, a "distant relative" of the Youngers, not far north of the Osage River ford at Roscoe. While they were asking the old man directions, two of the men they were seeking overheard their every word. Jim Younger, second of the brothers, and John, the fourth, were crouched by the second-story window just over their heads.

The lawmen were nearing the McFerrin place, not half a mile away, when they heard horses' hooves behind them. Cocking the shotgun he carried, John Younger called for the three to halt. Taken by surprise, two obeyed; the third, farther on, spurred his horse and managed to escape. After a lightning exchange, three men lay dead: the deputy, the other Pinkerton, and John Younger.

It was but a typical incident of the "outlaw years"—the desperate decade while the Radical rage spent itself in such grotesqueries as the Pinkertons' siege and fire-bombing of the James farm home, the maiming of Jesse's mother and murder of his nine-year-old brother, and finally the murky, unsavory "execution" of Jesse himself in his own home in 1882 by Bob Ford—paid off and hastily pardoned by Republican Governor Thomas T. Crittenden.

But the weary ordeal of the Bushwhackers of the Border—Missouri's Thirty Years' War—was gradually, at last drawing to a close. Already the hated Ironclad Oath—opposed even by leading Unionists—had been repealed in 1870; the national Liberal Republican movement had its birth in the struggle of Missouri moderates to repeal the unnatural oath. If "Reconstruction" had begun early in Missouri, so at least could "Redemption," the name given to the return of society's "natural leaders" to their rightful places. Not a year after John Younger's death, when a new Constitutional Convention met, it contained more members of Confederate than Union background! Osceola—the raped Osceola of 1861, which recently had cold-shouldered those doomed detectives—saw itself vindicated when the Convention named as chairman Waldo P. Johnson, ex-U. S. Senator from Osceola, ex-Confederate senator from Arkansas: an exemplary "natural leader" *redivivus*. The Constitution of 1875—under which "loyal" Missouri instantly elected ex-Confederate officers to high positions—remained the state's basic law down into living memory. In reaction to the rampant Radical activism and fiscal irresponsibility, the new Constitution "drastically curbed any potential tendency by the state to be profligate in matters of taxes, debt, and lending." Approval by two-thirds of the electorate was required on bond issues—a restriction still bemoaned by "progressives," who damn the conservative document as "a laissez faire tract, suspicious and distrustful of legislatures, [that] placed hampering restrictions on government, cut taxes severely, and starved tax-supported public services." Just so!

And the new regime set about closing the books on the time of troubles by offering the outlaws amnesty—"quarter," at long last.

For many, of course, it was too late. From the depths to which they'd been driven the "Dead Men" could not now be brought back. Released from prison long after the Northfield debacle, Jim Younger, ever the grim realist, bitterly slew his last victim—himself.

The successful, negotiated surrender of Frank James to Governor Crittenden, six months after Jesse's death, symbolized the return-from-the-grave grudged the lucky few, those who enjoyed notoriety —what a later time would call "name recognition."

In Nevada, where Frank moved in 1885, he was matter-of-factly made welcome. Why he should have picked this particular Border town in which to try and settle down is unclear. He was hardly the only ex-Bushwhacker to do so, however. George Maddox, Quantrill's chief scout during the Lawrence raid (and secretary of the band's postwar organization), managed a low-profile transition to the ways of peace in the erstwhile "Bushwhacker capital." William

Greenwood became a peaceful Moundville farmer. John Brown returned to his Sheldon area home. And it says much for the public regard for ex-Bushwhackers that, once ex-Confederates got back their voting rights, Henry Taylor was reelected sheriff!

On the other side of the ledger, James A. "Dick" Liddil, "a former Quantrillian" and James gang recruit, in 1876 had come to live in Nevada, home of his prominent, respected father.

The following year he was arrested and tried for horse-stealing in the Vernon County circuit court and drew a ten-year prison term, but mysteriously served only two years. His career with the James gang climaxed in the daring train holdup near Gallatin, Missouri, in 1881, resulting in two deaths and the governor's offer of tempting rewards for the capture of the suspected ringleaders Jesse and Frank James. Liddil—"a dashing, handsome fellow with dreamy blue eyes and a way with women"—was friendly with (among others) Martha Bolton, a young widow who "had a reputation as a rather loose woman." She also had two brothers, gang members Charley and Bob Ford. All three men, it seems, now decided to try bettering their own fortunes at their chief's expense.

Missouri politics and the issue of the outlaws were hopelessly intertwined. Crittenden, though seemingly decent and honest, had been put in office by the powerful railroad interests and the hardline Union faction that controlled Missouri through most of the postwar years. The ex-Confederate faction, rapidly regaining its influence, looked on the outlaws as victims of the war, more sinned against than sinning, and deserving of lenient treatment.

In April, 1882, the Fords, seemingly with some kind of secret understanding with the governor, came calling on Jesse James in the little St. Joseph home where he was living with his family as "Mr. Howard." As Jesse, his guns off, stood on a chair dusting a picture, Bob Ford put a bullet in the back of his head.

Frank James, quietly living under an alias in the East, realistically saw his brother's death as signaling or symbolizing the end of the outlaw era. Six months later, sided by John N. Edwards, General Jo Shelby's fiery adjutant, now editor of the unapologetically "unreconstructed" *Kansas City Times,* Frank surrendered to the governor in the latter's office. Despite the many charges outstanding against the outlaw who had "come in from the cold," Missouri hailed him as a hero. His train trip to Independence, where he was to be held for trial in the Gallatin affair, was a triumphal progress. "Had the train stopped long enough," one editor said, "he would have been given an ovation at every station."

Whether Frank actually fired the fatal shot during the Gallatin raid was never the real issue in the 1883 trial. The martyred Jesse's brother had become a symbol of the "Lost Cause," a pawn in the seesaw between the generally ex-Confederate Democrats and the largely Unionist Republicans—an angle Frank's eminent lawyers played to the hilt. General Jo Shelby, Missouri's most beloved hero, created a sensation by turning up in court somewhat the worse for drink and asking the judge's permission (denied) to "shake hands with an old soldier"—meaning the defendant.

Even more sensational was the appearance of Governor Crittenden himself—as a witness for the defense! Dick Liddil, the governor testified, had first told him Jesse, not Frank, had fired the crucial shot at Gallatin. So much for Liddil, on whose word the state's case hung. Since a convicted felon's testimony was inadmissible under Missouri law, the prosecution had had to stoop to tortuous reasoning. The judge had finally ruled that Liddil's release constituted a pardon, which wiped out his convict status.

The jury, all the same, was unconvinced. After hearing from Crittenden, "No one believed that Liddil was anything more than a traitor to his friends, a man whose word was not to be trusted." And anyhow, likely no ex-Confederate of Frank's stature could've been convicted of anything in the political climate of 1880s Missouri. The last charges against Frank were dropped in 1885.

Frank then had to decide what to do with the rest of his life. The sour taste left by Crittenden's collusion in the killing of Jesse James had contributed to his electoral replacement by John S. Marmaduke—ex-Union general replaced by ex-Confederate general! Reportedly the new governor advised Frank to "stay away from fast horses, get a job and remain out of sight for a year."

Frank heeded the advice by moving to Nevada, where he'd been offered a job in McGowan and Jordan's shoe store; Robert J. McGowan, his employer, had served with the near-Bushwhacker John Hunt Morgan. Aided by "sincere admirers," he bought "a neat little house at 520 South Cedar from the Methodist Church for $1200." Frank, his wife Annie, and their six-year-old son Robbie lived in the house for some five or six years. Acquaintances characterized

Annie James as "a pleasant, pretty little woman who was not inclined to be neighborly." The ex-outlaw himself, "a slender, sandy-haired man, minded his own business, took the family to church on Sundays, and worked during the week at McGowan and Jordan's shoe store." Anything but a clerk by temperament, he served the store primarily as a celebrity "drawing card." He also acted as a race starter for county fairs near and far. His idlest daily doings regularly made the newspaper's society column.

Often overlooked, it seems, is the fact that many of these reviled "incorrigibles", the Jameses among them, had managed, in the midst of their most "outlaw" years, to marry and lead conventional, "respectable" family lives, and once they were given the chance did make the wrenching adjustment to the ways of peace and law. Released from prison in chilly Minnesota, Cole Younger enjoyed a brief renaissance as a lecturer and Wild West showman, for a time in partnership with Frank James.

Other ex-Bushwhackers had it far harder. Many were unruly spirits by disposition as well as experience; they found postwar life "drab and diminished." Not all were well-known enough, or canny enough, to "market" themselves like James and Younger, and many had trouble making a living. In respectability-obsessed late-Victorian days, the "outlaw" stigma clung to them, even though most Missourians, at least at heart, saw them as heroes. In the folk memory, there were no distinctions between Bushwhackers and other Confederates—or if there were, time tended to heal them, even as it mellowed the past's bitterer divisions. The turn of the century was a time of reconciliations: of joint Union-Confederate reunions; of the return of captured Confederate battle flags; of public school children—including blacks—enjoying Rebel holidays. Recenter years have seen the Federal government furnishing gravemarkers for Confederates—even Bloody Bill Anderson—and Kansas returning Quantrill's bones to Missouri for burial. When ex-Quantrillite John Brown of Sheldon died in 1940, his obituary unashamedly, almost proudly recalled his part in the Lawrence raid.

Not till the wartime generation itself had wholly passed from the scene did "victor's history" begin to prevail. By the 1950s historical amnesia, that perennial human failing, had taken its toll, and in their ignorance—aggravated by the "civil rights" feeding frenzy —the grandchildren of Bushwhackers, indeed of all Confederates, might well find themselves trashing their own ancestors.

If the Bushwhackers "faded away" like all old soldiers, however, the Border itself showed a surprising persistence. While the farthest West was being swamped with settlers and organized into territories and states, the southern rump of the old "Indian Territory" had been left behind as the Last Frontier. Between Kansas and Texas no writ of state or territory ran. In this no-man's-land, post-Civil War outlaws from all the surrounding jurisdictions found final refuge, and so furnished the peculiar niche in history of Isaac C. Parker, late of Missouri, who from 1875 to 1896 presided over the Federal Court for the Western District of Arkansas having jurisdiction over the Indian Territory, and gained notoriety as the "Hanging Judge." Not till 1896, when tribal "governments" began to be done away with and judicial districts substituted, did law west of the Border approximate that to the east; and not till 1907 did statehood come to a combined Indian and white Oklahoma.

The Border had its effect even on the Cattle Kingdom. In the years just after the Civil War, the hostility of well-settled Missouri and Arkansas forced the famous cattle trails westward into sparsely settled Kansas. In the late 1860s, local alarm over the spread of Texas cattle fever, plus the westering of the railroads, effectively ended the old trail routes to Sedalia and Westport.

A further quirk prolonged the Border's life. Ripsnorting frontier Kansas had become one of the first states to try total prohibition of alcoholic beverages; and the mid-twentieth century, long after the national experiment's demise, found both Kansas and Oklahoma doggedly battling to stay "dry." Arkansas and Missouri, on the other hand, had gone back to being legally as well as actually soaking "wet." Lo, the old Border was the frontline in a new kind of war, with Missouri bootleggers and Ozarks moonshiners pitted against Kansas, Oklahoma, and Federal agents for the great profits realizable from illicit hooch. Shades of the old "Whiskey Road"! History had come full circle! Not till the 1950s when the two western states gave up and went "wet" did this last anomaly disappear.

Memory of the original and basic Border distinction, however, often is cloudy. As noted above, post-Civil War historical writers belonged to that national "establishment" dominated by the war's only real winners, the profiteers who'd garnered the great fortunes and the demagogues the great political careers of the day. Scholars

—never noted for courage or independence—toed the partyline: Confederate regulars might be excused, if not quite forgiven (as long as "reconciliation" remained politically expedient); but Bushwhackers weren't soldiers, they were outlaws, psychopaths, minions of Satan. One must search hard for "the other side," told only in buried smalltown newspaper columns and crudely printed or manuscript memoirs, diaries, and letters—the "underground press" of the period. At this writing that "other side" shows signs of coming back to life; even latterday Jayhawkers are having second thoughts. Truth's enemy today isn't so much "victor's history"—still officially in the saddle—as simply ignorance, historical amnesia.

One's initial impulse may be to applaud this fuzzing or forgetting of a past most memorable for its hatreds and free-for-all fights. Yet this is as much as to say that the issues behind those passions and battles—and the lessons they left for us, we can only pray—aren't worth remembering, or remembering *aright.* It's as much as to say that it all happened, literally, for nothing.

And this the heart, husbanding of the least scrap of human hope, must reject. The Civil War in western Missouri witnessed an unprecedented trampling of the very values all Americans most profess to cherish—this is why it's to the point to speak of a "lost cause." The noblest cause can always be lost, without that "eternal vigilance" our forefathers warned us is its price. It's not enough to kid ourselves that our national history's been a glorious march ever onward and upward, with never a slip nor a hitch. As George Caleb Bingham said of his polemical Reconstruction-era paintings, they would "illustrate to future generations an ignoble period of our State's history." "May the American people never forget. . . ." For history has a habit of repeating itself, and those forgetful of the past are fairly foredoomed to repeat its mistakes.

## ILLUSTRATION CREDITS

Page 1. Outline Map of U.S., showing the Border and the Timberline. *Bushwhacker Museum.*

3. Map of The Border. *Bushwhacker Museum.*

13. "Border Ruffians Going Over To Wipe Out Lawrence," in 1856. *State Historical Society of Missouri.*

24. Marais des Cygnes Massacre. *Kansas State Historical Society.*

25. The Hicklins Confront John Brown. *Terry Patterson.*

37. The Burning of Osceola. *Border Outlaws,* J. W. Buel, 1882.

45. Union Soldiers Pillaging in Missouri. *Frank Leslie's Illustrated Newspaper,* Sept. 28, 1861. *State Historical Society of Missouri.*

48. Quantrill's Men. *State Historical Society of Missouri.*

61. "Back Home, April, 1865," by Tom Lea, in Pleasant Hill (Mo.) Post Office. *Pleasant Hill Times.*

69. "Order No. 11," George Caleb Bingham. *State Historical Society of Missouri.*

72. The Killing of John Younger. *Border Outlaws,* J. W. Buel, 1882.

# A NOTE IN LIEU OF NOTES

**"Note this before my notes: There's not a note of mine that's worth the noting."—*Shakespeare*.**

The bemusement of some historians with footnotes and other scholarly stage-rigging is part of their overall effort to turn the venerable story-telling art of history into a "science."

It should be obvious that direct quotes are used in the present work for "literary" more than scholarly reasons—not to establish "facts" but for effect: for atmosphere, euphony, or concision.

For the "facts," as this writer sees it, are not at issue. What took place in Western Missouri in the Civil War period is well-known and even agreed upon. No new "fact" is likely to turn up to revolutionize the existing picture. What remains is to apply reason and common sense to the wealth of "facts" already in our possession.

Books go on being cranked out telling *what* happened, with little or no thought given, it seems, to *why*. The sins of the Bush-whackers are recycled ever anew, but the motives behind them never examined in the light of human behavior as a whole.

"Factual" historians shy from drawing the obvious conclusions from their "facts"—instead simply lugging in the received opinions out of the blue. They lay out the provocations to which Missourians were subjected, but then wax righteously indignant that they were so human as to let themselves be provoked.

Academics who previewed the first edition of this work had much to say about the quantity or quality of the footnotes, the sources. If they got around to the text at all, the thesis, it was merely to pronounce it hopelessly biased, and "parochial."

History, in the finer sense, probably is always "parochial." The sophisticated Athenians could no longer write like homely Homer—men had already stopped believing in his kind of truth; though two thousand years later Schliemann found Troy by heeding *The Iliad*. And *John Brown's Body* has been called our best Civil War history. What Sophocles or Milton might have made of Missouri's pride and fall and punishment! But we leave history to historians.

# INDEX

89

Mayfield, Sallie, 60
Methodists, 21
Mexican War, 40
Mexico, 71
Michigan, 15
Military Bill, 40
Military Road, Great, 9
Mine Creek, Kan., Battle of, 70, 71
Minneapolis, Minn., 9
Mississippi, 47, 52, 60
Mississippi River, 8, 9, 38, 46, 51, 52
Missouri, 1-21 passim, 24, 25, 37, 43, 49, 53
Missouri Compromise, 14, 16
Missouri River, 9, 12, 14, 42, 45, 46
Missouri State Guard (Confed.), 58
Missouri State Militia (Fed.), 43, 51, 54
Modrel, William, 70
Monegaw Springs, Mo., 78
Moneka, Kan., 32
Monroe, Pres. James, 8
Montevallo Academy, 62, 76
Montevallo, Mo., 42, 61, 62
Montevallo Township, 61
Montgomery, James, 18, 22, 23, 26, 30, 36, 44, 45
Moore's Branch, 64
Morgan, Gen. John Hunt, 53, 81
Mormonism, 21
Morse, Rev. Jedidiah, 7, 8
Nagel, Paul C., 21
Napoleonic Wars, 48
Nebraska, 17, 19, 26
Neosho, Mo., 41
Neosho River, 8
Nevada, Mo., 42, 44, 63, 64, 65, 75, 79, 81
New England, 14, 15
*New York Post*, 29
*New York Tribune*, 20, 32
Newtonia, Mo., Battle of, 70
Nonpartisan League, 21
Northfield, Minn., 77, 79
Northwest Conspiracy, 47
Ohio, 53
Oklahoma, 4, 68, 83
Olathe, Kan., 57
Ontario, 32
Order Number Eleven, 68, 69
Order Number Ten, 67

Order Number Thirty-two, 53
Ordinance of Secession, 41
Oregon, 14
Osage Indians, 4, 9
Osage River, 5, 6, 23, 46, 58
Osawatomie, Kan., 27
Osceola, Mo., 45, 46, 62, 67, 77, 79
Ozarks, 47, 77
Page, Walter Hines, 72
Papinsville, Mo., 45
"Parallels", John Brown's, 32
Parker, Judge Isaac C., 83
Parkville, Mo., 46
Partisan Ranger Act, 54
Pea Ridge, Ark., Battle of, 47, 59
Pierce, Pres. Franklin, 18
Pike, Capt. Zebulon M., 5, 7
Pinkerton, Alan, 32
Pinkerton Detective Agency, 78
Plains Proper, 4
Planter's House, 40
Platte County, Mo., 17
Pleasant Hill, Mo., 46
Potawatomie Creek, 27, 35
Potawatomie Massacre, 27
Prairie Plains, 4
Price, Gen. Sterling, 40, 42, 43, 44, 46, 47, 51, 54, 56, 58, 69
Pride's Purge, 40
Prohibitionism, 21, 83
Pugh, Maj. A. J., 63
Puritans, 26
Quantrill, William Clarke, 53, 55, 58, 59, 67, 68, 71
Radicals, 20, 26, 46, 50, 53, 73, 74, 75, 76, 78, 79
Reconstruction, 71, 73, 77, 79
Redemption, 79
Redfield, Abraham, 10
Redlegs, 68
Redpath, James, 20, 33
Red River, 9
Religion, 6, 39
Republican Party, 15, 16, 19, 20, 36, 73, 78, 81
Revolutionary War, 1
Reynolds, Lt. Gov. Thomas C., 41
Richland Township, 70
Richmond, Va., 47, 56

# SUGGESTIONS FOR FURTHER READING

Brownlee, Richard S. *Gray Ghosts of the Confederacy: Guerrilla Warfare in the West 1861-1865.* Baton Rouge, La: Louisiana State University Press, 1958.

Buresh, Lumir F. *October 25 and the Battle of Mine Creek.* Kansas City: Lowell Press, 1977.

Dyer, Robert L. *Jesse James and the Civil War in Missouri.* Columbia, Mo.: University of Missouri Press, 1994.

Fellman, Michael. *Inside War: The Guerrilla Conflict in Missouri During the American Civil War.* NY: Oxford University Press, 1989.

Goodrich, Thomas. *Black Flag: Guerrilla Warfare on the Western Border 1861-1865.* Bloomington: Indiana University Press, 1995.

Goodrich, Thomas. *War to the Knife: Bleeding Kansas 1854-1861.* Mechanicsburg, Pa.: Stackpole Books, 1998.

Leslie, Edward E. *The Devil Knows How to Ride: The True Story of William Clarke Quantrill and his Confederate Raiders.* New York: Random House, 1996.

Malin, James C. *John Brown and the Legend of Fifty-six.* New York: Haskell House Publishers, Ltd., 1971.

Monaghan, Jay. *Civil War on the Western Border 1854-1865.* Boston: Little Brown & Co., 1955.

Oates, Stephen B. *To Purge This Land With Blood: A Biography of John Brown.* Amherst: University of Massachusetts Press, 1970.

Phillips, Christopher. *Damned Yankee: The Life of Gen. Nathaniel Lyon.* Columbia, Mo.: University of Missouri Press, 1990.

Piston, W. G., & Hatcher, R. W. III. *Wilson's Creek.* Chapel Hill, N. C.: University of North Carolina Press, 2000.

Scott, Otto. *The Secret Six: The Fool as Martyr* [John Brown]. Columbia, S. C.: Foundation for American Education, 1979.

Settle, William A., Jr. *Jesse James Was His Name.* Columbia, Mo.: University of Missouri Press, 1966.

Thelen, David. *Paths of Resistance: Tradition and Dignity in Industrializing Missouri.* New York: Oxford University Press, 1986.

Welch, G. Murlin. *Border Warfare in Southeastern Kansas 1856-59.* Pleasanton, Kan: Linn County Historical Society, 1977.